This Book may be kept

FOURTEEN DAYS

A fine of TWO CENTS will be charged for each day
the Book is kept over time.

Jan 6 '59			
Jan 6 '59			
Feb 6 '59			
Jan 19 '61			
Jan 22 '64			
Feb 22 '67			
Nov 27 '72			
May 19 '75			

Library Bureau Cat. No. 1137.24

Ancient Peoples and Places

DENMARK

General Editor

DR GLYN DANIEL

DR GLYN DANIEL *Ancient Peoples and Places*

DENMARK

BEFORE THE VIKINGS

Ole Klindt-Jensen

73 PHOTOGRAPHS

15 LINE DRAWINGS

AND A MAP

FREDERICK A. PRAEGER

PUBLISHERS

BOOKS THAT MATTER

15 WEST 47 STREET · NEW YORK 36

© THAMES AND HUDSON LONDON 1957
PRINTED IN GREAT BRITAIN
BY JARROLD AND SONS LTD
NORWICH

TRANSLATED FROM THE DANISH
BY EVA AND DAVID WILSON

THIS IS VOLUME FOUR IN THE SERIES
ANCIENT PEOPLES AND PLACES

CONTENTS

ILLUSTRATIONS

Foreword

This book on Danish prehistory covers the period up to the advent of the Vikings, when the literary sources become sufficiently numerous for us to speak of a historic period. The Viking era in Denmark and the other Scandinavian countries is discussed by Holger Arbman in a separate volume in the 'Ancient Peoples and Places' series. The reader should bear in mind that the Romans did not reach Scandinavia, and that their influence was therefore appreciably less marked in Den-mark than in Great Britain.

I am indebted to Dr Glyn Daniel for his helpful advice while I was working on this short summary of a long cultural development. I also wish to thank Mr and Mrs David Wilson for their excellent rendering of the text.

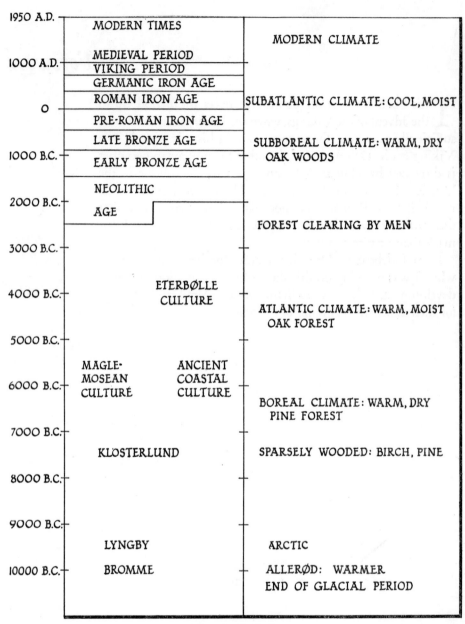

1950 A.D.	MODERN TIMES		MODERN CLIMATE
1000 A.D.	MEDIEVAL PERIOD		
	VIKING PERIOD		
	GERMANIC IRON AGE		
0	ROMAN IRON AGE		SUBATLANTIC CLIMATE: COOL, MOIST
	PRE-ROMAN IRON AGE		
	LATE BRONZE AGE		SUBBOREAL CLIMATE: WARM, DRY
1000 B.C.	EARLY BRONZE AGE		OAK WOODS
2000 B.C.	NEOLITHIC AGE		
3000 B.C.			FOREST CLEARING BY MEN
4000 B.C.		ETERBØLLE CULTURE	
5000 B.C.			ATLANTIC CLIMATE: WARM, MOIST OAK FOREST
6000 B.C.	MAGLE-MOSEAN CULTURE	ANCIENT COASTAL CULTURE	
7000 B.C.			BOREAL CLIMATE: WARM, DRY PINE FOREST
8000 B.C.	KLOSTERLUND		SPARSELY WOODED: BIRCH, PINE
9000 B.C.			
10000 B.C.	LYNGBY		ARCTIC
	BROMME		ALLERØD: WARMER END OF GLACIAL PERIOD

Periods and related climates.

Introduction

A HUNDRED AND FIFTY years ago on the 22nd of May 1807, by the command of Christian VII, King of Denmark, the Royal Commission for the Preservation of Antiquities was founded in Copenhagen. Its object was the preservation of ancient monuments and the collection of national antiquities; and in 1816 a young man, Christian J. Thomsen, was appointed as its secretary. With energy and imagination Thomsen created from the finds which poured into the Commission the nucleus of the Royal Museum for Nordic Antiquities, from which sprang the present National Museum of Copenhagen. Known colloquially as the Old Nordic Museum, with lecture tours conducted by the curator himself, it soon became one of the most popular attractions of Copenhagen. Thomsen lectured brilliantly about the antiquities in the museum and the prehistory they represented; linking past with present, he would place a heavy gold ring round the neck of a child and make prehistory live in the minds of his audience.

An acute observer, Thomsen was the first scholar to distinguish the three ages of prehistory, the Stone, Bronze and Iron Ages. Many years before he published his conclusions, he had arranged the exhibition of antiquities in the Old Nordic Museum according to this sequence. The system, which for some time was the subject of dispute, was arrived at by observing different antiquities repeatedly found in association with each other.

The second great personality of Danish archaeology was J. J. A. Worsaae, a man of different temperament but no less enthusiasm. He became aware of the importance of looking at the objects in their natural surroundings and travelled about the countryside studying and excavating the visible remains of

Plate 3

Plate 1

Fig. 1

ancient man. He subdivided the archaeological periods established by Thomsen, dividing both the Stone and Bronze Ages
into two. In the Stone Age, for instance, he distinguished an
earlier phase, typified by the coarse tools of the 'kitchen-
middens', and a later phase typified by polished flint tools and
megalithic tombs. He travelled widely in Europe, being a
frequent visitor, for instance, to the British Isles; and studied
prehistoric cultures in a wide context which enabled him to
draw conclusions concerning the archaeological characteristics
of different areas. His writings, based on these investigations, are
vivid and thorough. The fact that his first book appeared during
the rise of nationalism, just before the middle of the nineteenth
century, colours his work, without detracting from its balance.
He emphasized forcefully that the prehistory of Denmark (the
title of one of his books) was the condition precedent to the
later cultural development of the country. In the nationalistic
temper of the period such emphasis added to the popularity of
prehistoric archaeology.

A new institution, the Inspectorate for the Preservation of
Ancient Monuments, was created under the leadership of
Worsaae. From this institution Worsaae carried out a survey
of the ancient monuments and prehistoric material of Denmark
and inaugurated excavations throughout the country. In 1879
he became Director of the Old Nordic Museum and brought
the Inspectorate for the Preservation of Ancient Monuments
with him; this gave the National Museum a sphere of work and
influence wider than that of most other large museums.

Plate 2

The heir to Thomsen and Worsaae was Sophus Müller, an
acute scholar and a great administrator. For sixty years between
the 1870's and his death in 1934 his published work consoli-
dated the foundations upon which the study of Danish prehistory is based. He did not spend a great deal of time in the
field, relying rather on the experience of his excellent helpers.
On the basis of the work of these helpers he was able (in 1897)

to draw up an excavational programme for the National Museum which demanded accurate planning and description. This plan emphasized the importance of establishing the relationship between the different structures excavated, and the necessity of photographing important details. Sophus Müller

Fig. 1. Worsaae, in State Archaeologist's uniform, supervising the ex- cavation of Danevirke near Slesvig in 1861. Drawing by M. Petersen.

published a large number of excavation reports, often in colla- boration with his colleagues, and sometimes with natural scientists. His book *Vor Oldtid* ('Our Prehistory'), published in 1897, summarized clearly and vividly the state of archaeological knowledge at that time.

The scholars of this century have built on these firm founda- tions. This book is concerned with their work and with the re- sults which they have produced. The work of this century is excellently summarized, for those who read Danish, in the three volumes of Johannes Brøndsted's *Danmarks Oldtid*, published between 1938 and 1940.

Chapter I

The Palaeolithic

THE ICE AGE AND THE FIRST HUNTERS

THREE TIMES DURING the hundred thousand years of the Ice Age, the ice crept southwards over the whole of Denmark. Three times it melted, retreated and gave way to exuberant vegetation and to forests inhabited by animals. Fifteen thousand years ago, the ice finally retreated. During the Ice Age, it extended over three-quarters of the length of Jutland, moulding in the process the physical features of Denmark. Boulders, sand and clay, carried in the frozen ice cap, were scattered over the face of the country. Sand was washed out through the openings of the glacier over West Jutland and clay was spread over East Jutland and the islands. The weight and movement of the ice striated the rocks of Bornholm. The country became level, with gently rolling hills.

There were, therefore, three periods during which the country could have been inhabited by man; but it is only recently that the presence of man has been recognized in one of the warm (interglacial) periods of the Ice Age, although the evidence had been available for half a century. The zoologist Ulrik Møhl, in the course of his examination of Ice Age fauna, investigated an inconspicuous collection of fallow-deer bones which were dated to the period of the last interglacial, about 50,000 B.C. When he tried to glue the fragments together he discovered that the bones had been split with a hard chopping tool, in order to extract the marrow. Since this could only have been done by human agency and since the fallow-deer is unknown in Denmark after the Ice Age, the conclusion that man lived in Denmark during this period is inescapable. It was probably Neanderthal man who hunted and killed the fallow-deer in the forest of this period. Although in Denmark we have what may only be the remains of one meal, we know enough about Neanderthal man from other sources to enable us to reconstruct a little of his way of life. He lived in tents and had certain characteristic flint tools. These people, with their prominent brow ridges, their low foreheads and powerful jaws, knew how to obtain and use fire; they hunted game and collected plants and fruit. While the forest covered the country they managed to obtain their living from the natural sources around them but, as the ice moved forward and tundra replaced forest, they became extinct.

Only when the ice had finally melted away and conditions became more favourable, do we again find traces of hunters as they followed the wild animals moving to the new pastures in the north. The climate was cool but the summers warm enough for a rich vegetation of hardy plants to germinate; bedstraw, hepatica, bear-berry, arctic birch and many kinds of grass flourished in these conditions. In the later, milder, transitional periods (the Bølling and Allerød periods) open birch forests appeared.

In the colder periods the summer temperature varied between 46° and 50° F. and during the Allerød period the temperature rose to 55° and 57° F. Despite the great length of time, amounting to several thousand years, covered by the Late Glacial period, traces of habitation by hunters are rare. It seems probable, however, that the country was inhabited by only a few groups of hunters who needed large tracts of land to provide them with sufficient food.

Occasionally tools, such as a variety of knife made from reindeer-antler, have been found that can be assigned to the Late Glacial period. The people of this period may have belonged to a group of hunters of the Hamburgian culture, which is well known in the areas south of the Danish border at the extreme south of Jutland. They used tools of flint; arrow-heads, scrapers and different types of burin, as well as tools of antler

and bone (cf. Fig. 3b and a). The burin was a sharp/
pointed tool with a transverse edge and was used to cut long
grooves in bone and antler in order to extract splinters from the
hard outer core; for undercutting these splinters another
typical tool, known as a *zinke,* was used, which has a curved
beak/like profile.

Fig. 2. Tanged arrow/head from Bromme (½ actual size).

The hunters of the earliest settlement site found on Danish
soil, at Bromme in West Zealand, though distinct from the
hunters of the Hamburgian sites, were at an equally advanced
cultural stage. The settlement was situated on a peninsula
jutting out into a small shallow lake. The situation of a Stone
Age site near a lake is always a happy coincidence for the
archaeologist on account of the waste material which can be
found under special conditions. Stone Age man could no more
resist the splash of objects thrown into water than can his
modern counterpart; rejected and superfluous objects would
thus find their way into the lake and, if the soil contains lime
and certain other chemicals, even bone and antler is preserved.
Unfortunately, although the conditions at Bromme were
favourable, only a small number of bones was preserved.

The summer countryside must have been very inviting
during this period (the Allerød period). Yellow squill, blue
cornflower and other flowers shimmered in the rich grass. In
the open landscape were trees: birch, aspen, pine and the rowan
tree, whose young shoots attracted hungry elks and giant red
deer. By the side of the lake or river the beavers would gnaw at
the base of the trees, busily building their dams. The horse and
the reindeer grazed on the open plain some distance from the
lake. Such game was rich quarry for the hunter; from the skins
were made clothes and tents; from the bones and antlers, tools;
from the sinews, rope; while from the meat, marrow, entrails
and brain came food. In order to kill the game and reap its
benefits the sharp, hard flint had to be flaked and chipped to
provide tools and weapons.

One of the commonest flint tools of this period is the tanged
arrow-head. To obtain this, a slender point, or flake, was struck
from a nodule of flint (the tip being sharp and unchipped) and
the point was then finely trimmed along its base and tied to the
haft, the trimming giving purchase to the binding cord.

Fig. 2

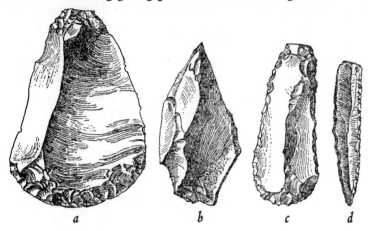

a   b   c   d

*Fig. 3. Flint objects from Klosterlund. From left to right: oval
scraper, burin, flake-scraper, microlith (all ¾ actual size).*

Once a reindeer had been killed, the hunter skinned the
animal with sharp flint flakes. The flakes which he used were
knife-like tools, irregularly shaped, but none the less effective.
They were struck from a core and some of them were trimmed,
or blunted, to make them easier to control in the hand; we may
presume that they were sometimes hafted. Such flakes are
almost as sharp as a modern knife.

Flakes of similar shape as well as small discoidal flints were
fashioned as scrapers and used to clean the inner side of the
skin (cf. Fig. 3a). Flakes chosen for this purpose were often
slightly curved in profile, the edge being trimmed away so as to
make a more acute angle. The angle of the trimming of the edge
of these scrapers is rather shallow, although the greater angle (so

common in the succeeding period) is occasionally to be seen. The trimmed edge is often curved, and in the case of the dis, coidal scrapers, only part of the edge is trimmed (cf. Fig. 3c).

Splinters were cut from bone and antler with the burins already mentioned. The burins of the Bromme people were rather clumsily made, the cutting edge being formed by one or two lateral blows to the flake which left a sloping transverse edge.

Other tools of the Bromme folk are awls, coarse pieces of flint with worn points, and 'block, scrapers' which are made from heavy flat, bottomed blocks of flint, the basal edge being finely trimmed and the undersides sometimes showing signs of wear (cf. Fig. 5c).

Exact parallels to this series of implements are not found out, side Denmark, but in general form and context the series is related to that found in North, west Germany (on such sites as Stellmoor and Pinneberg), in the Swiderian culture of Poland and on sites of the Aurignacian culture in Western and Central Europe, where the so, called *Font Robert* points from Périgordian sites are presumably prototypes of the Bromme arrowheads.

Charcoal from the Bromme settlement has been dated to about 10,000 B.C. by the well, known Carbon 14 method of dating, developed by atomic, scientists.

The Bromme culture survived for a considerable time, but the population of Denmark during this period must have been very small, as each small settlement needed a large hunting area in order to obtain the bare necessities of life. Perhaps only a few families wandered from place to place, but their descendants survived in Denmark for a thousand years.

The mild climate of the Allerød period gave way to less kind conditions; the tundra spread once more over the country, the elk and giant red deer retreated southwards, leaving the rein, deer, horse, wolf, lynx and fox behind. During this period we have a distinct culture named after the sites at Lyngby, in North Jutland, and Ahrensburg, near Hamburg in North Germany. For the first time, in Denmark, the axe is found. The axe of this culture consists of a long reindeer-antler on which a tine has been sharpened to a cutting edge. Several such axes have been found in Denmark and occasionally the tine is hollowed out to hold a sharp flint edge. One axe shows traces of wear from a cord which has been tied round it; similar tools with a similar cord arrangement were used quite recently in Alaska, but as we shall see below, they were not used for felling trees.

Plate 4

Of the pointed splinters cut from the reindeer-antler, one of the characteristic types has a double-edged point. In the latest tundra layer at Lyngby, a heavy arrow-head was found.

A settlement site of this period has been examined a little south of the Danish frontier, at Stellmoor, Holstein. Reindeer-antler axes and tanged arrow-heads were found on this site as well as harpoon-heads. Burins were not used to detach the splinters of bone or antler from the core; the splinters were detached by means of sharp blows from an antler axe.

Shoulder-blades, found at Stellmoor, which have been pierced by one or two accurate shots, provide interesting evidence of the penetrating power of an arrow. One of the strangest finds from this site was the skull of a reindeer which had been placed, presumably as an offering, on the end of a long pole: other reindeer had been killed and thrown into the bog. These offerings must be taken as a propitiation to the animals, or to the gods who gave good hunting.

CHAPTER II

The Mesolithic

THE FOREST PERIOD

AFTER A FINAL COOL INTERVAL, the ice ultimately receded and melted away to the north, leaving Denmark bounded by the sea on three sides. The forest spread over the country and the dark green pine became the commonest tree. In the clearings of the forest were grass and low bushes, and only the banks of the rivers and the shores of the sea were free from trees. In the forest lived game: elk, wild boar, bear, red deer and aurochs.

The hunters of this period lived near water; by the side of a lake or on the sea-shore. Occasionally settlements are found inland in a place with a wide vista, or on a sand or gravel subsoil.

Plate 6

We know very little about the settlements of these people but, on occasions, traces of a few simple huts have been found which give us an insight into their building technique. Investigation of their habitation sites has also demonstrated to us why they placed their settlements on the lakes. In the mild, dry climate of this period the large lakes were overgrown with reeds and peat, on which grew alder and birch. At Ulkestrup, on an island formed in this fashion a short distance out into the lake, a hut was built near to the fishing- and to the hunting-grounds. Just outside the hut stood a very large alder: but once when the hut was unoccupied the tree was blown down during a storm, badly damaging the hut as it fell. On excavation the floor was found to be well preserved; it consisted of large strips of birch-bark, nearly 6 feet long, 1 foot 6 inches wide and 1 inch thick, covering an area which measured 20 by 15 feet. On the floor were found branches of pine and, here and there, soft beds of bracken. In the centre of it was the hearth, a circular area nearly 5 feet across, containing sand, clay, ashes and charcoal.

On the floor was a two-inch layer of flint artifacts and hazel-nuts. The layer was strictly confined by the limits of the rectangle, save only towards the south-east where the hut faced the lake. Here the refuse layer continued outside the hut; indeed, much of the discarded material found by the archaeo-logists was recovered from an area that was then below the water-level. The door of the hut must, then, have faced towards the south-east, towards the lake; the boat was probably drawn up outside the door of the hut on top of the rubbish. From this we can see that the lake dominated the thoughts of the people. From it came their daily food and they could observe the comings and goings of the animals and birds through the open door of the hut.

The concentration of the artifacts and rubbish within the rectangular area of the floor shows that there were permanent, impenetrable walls surrounding the hut. The walls were probably light structures of wicker-work made out of rushes and reeds, but not bound with daub, as no trace of clay was found on the site. The walls were supported by a series of posts, as thick as a man's wrist. These posts were not found on all sides of the hut and it seems likely that a number of them were removed at some time after the hut was abandoned.

Certain finds indicate the time of the year during which the settlement was used. One young deer whose remains were found could not have been killed before June, and the hazel-nuts, of which many shells survive, would have been collected in the late summer.

The hut was therefore only used during the summer. The excavator carefully analysed the artifacts found in the hut and noticed that all the small flint points, known as microliths, exhibit exactly the same peculiarities of manufacture; this points to their having been made by the same man. It seems probable that only one family lived in the hut, although there was room for many more people.

One of the objects thrown out or abandoned by the people living in the hut was a beautifully carved paddle, nearly four feet in length, made from a plank of hazel wood. It has a long slender handle and a short wide blade—a typical paddle which corresponds to another Zealand bog-find at Holmegård. There was no trace of the boat; but if, as seems likely, it was made from skins stretched over a wooden framework, this would have quickly rotted away, leaving no trace. No boat from this period has been found; but it is possible too, that the Mesolithic boats were made from the trunks of trees, as they were in later periods.

Finds from other Danish bogs supply us with further information concerning these people. Despite the fact that the only tool they had for carving wood was a thin flint knife, they knew how to use it skilfully. The paddle we have just described demonstrates the quality of their work, as does a long-bow from Holmegård. This weapon tapers from its thick centre towards its ends; in the middle are two wide grooves to provide a grip for the hand. The bow was a powerful one, demanding, as modern copies have shown, a strong arm, and was well designed; had it been less substantially constructed it would have snapped. It was an effective weapon and was used, not only against the larger game, but also, as the bones found on certain sites show, against birds. The hunter was helped by dogs, of which there were two breeds, one large and one small.

During peat-cutting in the bog at Vig, North-west Zealand, a skeleton was found which tells a strange story of a Mesolithic hunt. The skeleton was that of a wild aurochs, a mighty animal with noble, curved horns. Twice it had cheated the hunters, the first time when arrows had penetrated deep into its flank, but on the second occasion it was more seriously wounded by arrows. It was strong enough, however, to escape through the forest and seek refuge in a small lake, where it swam until exhausted, its blood clouding the clear water; then, slowly and helplessly, it sank down into the mud which covered its wounded body pierced by death-dealing arrows.

The remains of plants and birds show that the settlement sites which have been excavated were largely inhabited during the summer months. Every autumn the hunters left the settle-ments, streams and lakes and went in search of new hunting-grounds. As in modern hunting communities, economy and subsistence were conditioned by the habits of the animals and by the state of the weather, a feature we have already noticed in the Ice Age.

In England at Star Carr, near Scarborough, a settlement was recently excavated which proved to belong to the same culture as the Middle Jutland site at Klosterlund. Side by side with harpoons and flint points found at this site were a number of curiously worked bone and antler fragments. Some of the frontal bones of red deer, for instance, to which the antlers were attached, were pierced by four holes. The holes indicate that the bone was tied on to something, and it seems most probable that it was carried by the hunter himself. Corroboration for such a theory is provided by a painting in one of the caves of the Western European Ice Age of a man with antlers on his head; we cannot, of course, tell whether the man used the antlers to attract his quarry or whether he was indulging in some magico-religious dance in which he imitated the animals and their movements.

At the present stage of our knowledge we cannot solve this problem; and it is perhaps doubtful whether the Mesolithic hunter was able to distinguish between a hunting ruse and a magic spell in his efforts to catch game. We must not, however, imagine that the hunter's life was completely occupied in catch-ing game and gathering food. Fine ornaments show that this people had an interest in things other than those necessary for bare subsistence. Their art largely comprises a scratched linear decoration of simple design, but occasionally we find represen-tations of human beings and animals executed in a naïve and original manner. Tools, weapons and ornaments of amber, bone or antler were covered with fine incised geometrical designs or more crudely executed drilled pit ornament. Occasionally they carved animals in the round, in a manner which shows a sensitive appreciation of the animal's form and characteristics. The identity of the bear at the top of Plate 5 is unmistakable and it is dated to this period by the fine incised ornament on its side; similarly the head of the elk (right centre) is well designed and is dated by the drilled bit ornament. More amusing, perhaps, are the representations of the human figure; Plate 5, bottom, for instance, shows a small group of figures incised on the heavy bone of an aurochs. It is possible to equate this group to a family, and it is certainly tempting to do so. To the right is a dignified figure, perhaps the father, with three other figures, the mother and two girls, inclined towards him: all these figures are cross-hatched, while to the left the son is depicted in quick motion, perhaps not sharing with the others the interest in the important person to the right.

The hunting culture remained unchanged for many thousand years but, although it survived into the second millennium B.C., several fundamental changes occurred during its long history.

The settlement site at Klosterlund in Middle Jutland, which is the oldest known settlement of the Maglemosean culture, has certain characteristic features. It was situated near a small lake which was surrounded by the birch trees so common in Denmark at this period (8–9000 years ago). Unfortunately the soil of the Klosterlund site had a low lime content and bones and antlers were not preserved. On the other hand, we are lucky to have the important contemporary site at Star Carr in Yorkshire which has yielded a lot of information about the cultural and economic conditions of this period. At this time Denmark was connected to England by a land bridge across the North Sea, a bridge formed of the Dogger Bank and other shallows, and the wandering hunters of this period could quite easily travel from

Plate 5

Plate 5

Star Carr to Klosterlund or vice versa. It was not many centuries after this that the sea submerged the land bridge and once
again separated Jutland from England.

The perforated deer frontlets from Star Carr have already
been mentioned but the site also produced other antlers which
were grooved longitudinally. From these antlers, splinters had
been carved, with burins, for later manufacture into harpoonheads and awls.

At Klosterlund and Star Carr we find the first proper flint
axes, made either from a core or from a flake. Here is the birth
of a type of tool which we shall see continuously in the pages
that follow: these axes are not very elegant but they are a very
characteristic feature of the culture (cf. Fig. 5a). The coreaxe
was made of a nodule of flint, chipped on both faces to produce
an oval tool with a sharp edge formed by a few skilful chipping
blows. This must be distinguished from the flakeaxe (cf. Fig.
5b), which was made from a large flake, with a sharp edge,
struck from a nodule or core of flint; the sharp edge was left
and the other sides were blunted until the axe was roughly
triangular in shape with heavily trimmed sides.

In Denmark we first meet the axe, a tool which has been of
vital importance in man's history, in the Mesolithic period, and
even in this crude form it could be used to fell trees.

Discoidal scrapers have been found at both Bromme and
Klosterlund and, although most of them are round, an
occasional oval example (with trimming at one end) is found.
Other types of scrapers are the blockscraper (formed of a core
of flint with short, steep trimming at its receding cuttingedge),
the planescraper (of similar form, but made from only part of
a core) and the flakescraper (the edge of which is usually convex, but occasionally concave).

The flakes, though rather coarse, are skilfully struck. Besides
being made into scrapers they were used in the manufacture of
burins, which are characterized by a strong edge in the middle

Fig. 3a

Fig. 5c

Fig. 3c

Fig. 3b

or to one side of the flake. They were also used as knives, with trimming along one edge, and as small saws, with serrated edges.

Fig. 3d

Small flakes were made into microliths, tiny tools trimmed along one or both sides. Some are triangular in shape, some lanceolate and a third common variety has trimming along one long side.

These small objects have a long history, stretching back into the Ice Age. They are common in the Late Palaeolithic period and are especially characteristic of the Western European Meso⁄lithic culture known as Tardenoisian. A few chance finds have shown us how these tiny blades were used. A wooden arrow, for instance, was found in a Scanian bog, with a shaft two feet nine inches in length, and about two⁄ or three⁄tenths of an inch thick. Attached to the tip of the shaft was found a microlith embedded in resin; this showed the impression of a second microlith, and the two together would have formed a barbed arrow⁄head. It is reasonable to suppose that the triangular micro⁄liths were designed to be used in this way, to barb the head of an arrow.

The Maglemosean culture is known in its classic form from finds in the Zealand bogs at Maglemose, near Mullerup (the first settlement site to be found and the one which gave its name to the culture), Sværdborg, Lundby, Holmegård and Åmosen. Differences are to be noticed between the types of objects found on these sites, but the differences are not far⁄reaching and are only to be expected in a culture that covers large areas and a considerable period of time. The material from Maglemose contains some clumsy flakes and simple lanceolate micro⁄liths, while the later finds from Sværdborg show a brilliant technique of flint⁄working, with slender, elegant flakes and many small microliths in a variety of forms, triangular, lanceo⁄late, trapezoid, etc. A variety of other tools has been found: core⁄axes, smaller flake⁄axes, scrapers and burins of shapes we

Fig. 4.
Triangular
microlith from
Sværdborg
(¾ actual size).

Fig. 4

Fig. 5a. Mesolithic flint implements: core-axe ($\frac{3}{4}$ actual size).

27

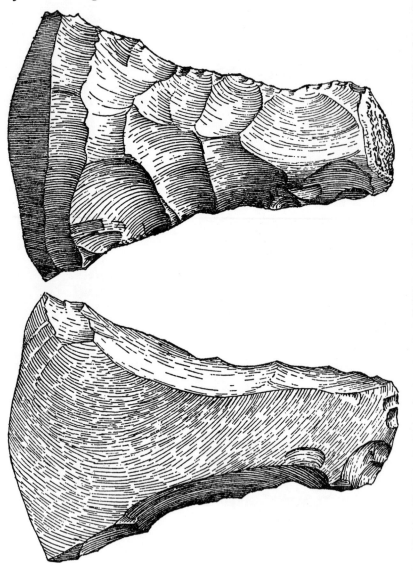

Fig. 5b. Flake-axe (actual size).

have already seen from Klosterlund, but executed in a finer technique. The flint-workers at Sværdborg were masters of their craft, but they also had at their disposal an excellent raw material, the Zealand flint, easily found in the moraines of the island.

Fig. 5c. Block-scraper (¾ actual size).
Plate 5

Of great interest is the large number of antler and bone tools; of these the most numerous are the points, or harpoon-heads, which have short barbs along one side. Less characteristic are points with large barbs or with a notched side. Occasionally, beautiful composite points are found with grooves along the sides, in which are inserted small flakes of flint, secured with resin.

Axe-blades were also made from deer-antler, the shaft-hole always being in the base of the axe and not, as in later periods, through the beam of the antler. In some instances the surface of the axe was smoothed and decorated with drilled pit ornamentation, while other axes retained the natural surface of the antler. The axes have a chisel-shaped cutting-edge or have a flake of a flint or a tooth inserted in a hollow to form a sharp edge. Another important tool was the chisel made out of a heavy long bone which had been given a transverse cutting-edge.

Among other tools and weapons, two types were especially popular; one was a pointed, hafted weapon of antler, and the other was a bone dagger. These objects were often decorated, and occasionally are covered with fine, intricate patterns that resemble embroidery. The long carved antler points have a shaft-hole at the thick end. The hunters who made them may well have been attempting to emulate the deer, who could do so much damage with their fine heads.

Fig. 5d. Rhomboid microlith, Ancient Coastal culture (¾ actual size).

Full use was made of bone and antler; a sawn-off trochlea made a useful polishing tool, the smaller tines of antler were used as strikers for flint-working and other pieces of bone were made into awls and fish-hooks.

An offshoot of the Maglemosean culture settled by the lakes

and along the streams and rivers of Jutland. Their settlements are found in characteristic positions, for example, on low sandy slopes just above the river banks, dry dwelling/places with a commanding view over the stream. The finds from most of these settlement sites comprise a small number of minor tools, evidence of a short stay in one place. Other sites were used from season to season and visited often. The settlements by the Gudenå, for instance, were also used in the later period and tools, transverse arrow/heads and large numbers of flake/axes, characteristic of the Ertebølle culture, were also found here.

Characteristic Maglemosean settlements have been found on the islands of Funen and Bornholm. The Bornholm sites, how/ever, exhibit some variant features; for example, one of the Bornholm groups is connected, by the tiny, elegant microliths, to the Zealand site of Sværdborg, but other sites form groups of a purely local character. Some settlements are sited along the banks of streams, while others are found on sand and gravel terraces just above sea/level; one site, strangely enough, is found high up in a rocky area overlooking the greater part of the north of the island. But, despite such freaks, it is true to say that the settlement sites of the Maglemosean people were carefully chosen; they were placed near the good hunting/ and fishing/ grounds.

At the same time as the Maglemosean culture flourished by the lakes, the sea coast was inhabited by a different people. Traces of them are rarely found, as their settlements have been drowned by the rising level of the sea. They differed from the Maglemosean people in many ways. Their material culture was characterized by rhomboid microliths and oblique arrow/heads, more closely related to the German Ahrensburg culture than to the slender microliths of the Maglemosean people. Occasionally the coastal people turned inland and settled by the lakes, as at Kongemose, West Zealand, where tools of antler and bone have been found. It is interesting to see that

Fig. 5d

these migrants used pointed weapons and ornamental decora
tion related to those of the Maglemosean culture.

The culture is known as the Early Coast, or Early Ertebølle, culture. It was first recognized during the excavation of the

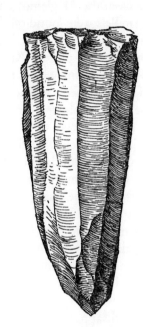

Fig. 5e. Flake-scraper.   *Fig. 5f. Flake-core.*

(Both ¾ *actual size.*)

Stone Age settlement site at Bloksbjerg to the north of Copen
hagen. The settlement was situated on a slope which faced towards a bog. While studying the finds from the site, the excavator noticed very definite differences between the material from the upper and lower levels. The objects found in the upper (later) levels corresponded exactly with material from the numerous 'kitchen-middens'; the material from the lower level,

Plate 7

31

however, was without close parallel. The botanists were able to analyse the pollen in the lower level and found that the vegetation had consisted of a pine and mixed oak forest. The dating was therefore certain: the lower level at Bloksbjerg represented an earlier settlement which could be placed in a stage between the Maglemosean and Ertebølle cultures. Eventually, parallels were found off the coast of Amager, at Dyrholmen in East Jutland, from Vedbæk in North Zealand and from many other places. At Dyrholmen there were several periods of settlement which present a very interesting feature. Each of the settlements was adjusted to the sealevel (as was also the case in Bloksbjerg), so that the oldest settlement was farthest out at a level of 7 feet above the present sealevel. Farther in, later tools were found at the 8–9 foot level and the latest tools were found higher up still at a height of 10½ feet. The site was obviously ideal for settlement, but each time the people returned the rising waterlevel forced them higher up the slope; it is thus possible to obtain comparative dating of the settlements from their distribution.

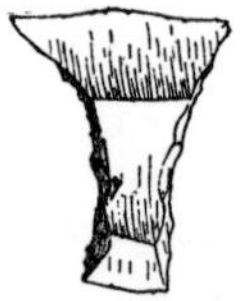

Fig. 6. Transverse arrowhead (¾ actual size).

The earlier and later phases of the Ertebølle culture are clearly distinguished by the form of the arrowheads: in the earlier phase the rhomboid microliths are of common occurrence; in the later phase, however, transverse arrowheads appear and the microliths disappear. Another indication is given by a comparison of the core and flakeaxes; in the early phase (as in the Maglemosean period) only a small number of flakeaxes occur while in the later phase the proportion of flakeaxes to core axes is conspicuously large. The earlier levels of an Ertebølle site produced barbed bone points and composite bone and flint points as well as keel scrapers, antler axes with a hafting hole through the base and other Maglemosean types. Later in the Ertebølle period these types become scarce or disappear completely. At this level the first pottery vessels appear, large vessels with a pointed base built up from strips of clay pressed

Fig. 5d

Fig. 6

Fig. 5a

together in a spiral band. The clay contains an admixture of gravel, perhaps to enable it to stand up to great heat. Owing to its shape, the vessel could not stand by itself, and had either to be embedded in sand or surrounded by stones (the stones may sometimes have been heated to help the cooking process).

Many of these settlements reveal a gradual change in the customs and conditions which governed life: a change coeval with the changing face of Denmark. The sea was still attacking the coast; banks of sand and gravel a little way inland testify to this day to the power of the sea at this period. The surface of the sea rose a number of feet above its present level not once, but probably three times, the last rise occurring in the Late Stone Age.

The study of this period of prehistory is in the melting-pot; new ideas compete with one another and the story is not yet clear. The botanist is bringing us new understanding of the beginnings of Neolithic settlement in Denmark through his study of the indestructible pollen which he finds in the bogs. The bogs can at times tell us of tools and farms but more of the influence of agriculture on nature, a knowledge of which is invaluable to the archaeologist. But first let us consider the origin of agriculture.

CHAPTER III

The Neolithic

THE COMING OF AGRICULTURE

A T A TIME WHEN SCANDINAVIA was still inhabited
by a population of hunters and fishers, a new people was
spreading from the South and the South-east over Central and
Western Europe. On the rich and fertile loess soil of this area
we find the first European agricultural communities whose
settlement sites have produced the distinctive rounded pottery
with linear decoration, that gives the *Bandkeramik* culture its
name. These settlement sites yield traces of long rectangular
houses, associated with smaller huts which may be interpreted
as granaries. From the animal remains found on such sites we
know that the first farmers had domesticated the cow, pig and
sheep and had begun to cultivate barley and the primitive
wheats, einkorn and emmer. Traces are also found of the
agricultural implements used by these people, simple saddle
querns for grinding corn and axe-like blades of hoes with
traces of wear along one side and at one end.

Agriculture had spread from the Middle East where, long
before the advent of the *Bandkeramik* culture in Europe, wild
plants had been selected and systematically cultivated in fields
near the settlement. With the domestication of animals and the
development of agriculture a new economy was created which
exploited nature in a revolutionary fashion. The Carbon 14
dating method has provided us with reasonably accurate dates
for the first appearance and development of agriculture in the
Western Hemisphere. Thus the earliest agricultural settlement
in the Elburz Mountains, by the Caspian Sea, is dated to about
5800 B.C.; in Mesopotamia, the Jarmo culture is dated to about
4700 B.C.; the *Bandkeramik* settlement near Magdeburg in
Germany dates from about 4200 B.C.; while the earliest known

34

Danish agricultural settlement (Muldbjerg I in West Zealand) is dated to about 2640 B.C., a date which is more or less con/ temporary with that of the Cortaillod culture of Switzerland.

There was therefore a gap of about fifteen hundred years between the first appearance of agriculture in Europe and its first appearance in Denmark. It is possible, however, that there was an earlier contact between Denmark and the *Bandkeramik* culture, for some of its distinctive axes have been found on Danish sites; yet these may have come from a later phase.

Archaeology recognizes two direct indications of the arrival of agriculture; the discovery on settlement sites of bones of domesticated animals and the discovery either of burnt grain or of impressions of grain in the fabric of pottery. Recently, in/ direct evidence of the arrival of agriculture has been provided by the study of pollen in the bogs outside the settlements, certain vegetational changes having been proved to be due to the practice of agriculture.

Traces of a widespread fire have been found at a certain level in many Danish bogs. Above this level, and therefore after the fire, the general vegetation is seen to change in character. New pollens are found: cereals, grasses and plantain such as thrive in pastures. Johannes Iversen, who first noticed this feature, came to the conclusion that forest fires were started by farmers in order to clear fields and pastures in the forest and his con/ clusion has been confirmed by the varieties of pollen, and by the bones of domesticated ox, found in this new horizon of the burnt level.

Many votive deposits of pottery are known from the earliest agricultural period. This Early Neolithic pottery was not properly recognized until large quantities were revealed by extensive peat/cutting during the Second World War. The *Early Neolithic period* in Denmark is divided into three phases, A, B and C, and this pottery is assigned to the earliest phase (A). This phase is connected, as indeed are the other two, with

Fig. 7

the Funnel-Necked Beaker culture of the Continental area south of the Baltic. Potsherds typical of this early group, with their distinctive rounded shape and out-turned rim (known as A-beakers), were excavated at Store Valby in the west of Zealand, and revealed impressions of grain.

Impressions of grain were also found on the characteristic A-beakers from Åmosen, a settlement site of the earliest farming culture. To the astonishment of the excavator, the tools and other objects found on this site, flake-axes, coarse sherds of pointed-based pottery and transverse arrow-heads, were characteristic of the Late Ertebølle culture. The local hunter/fisher population had evidently taken up farming and stock-raising. Bones of domesticated cow, sheep and goat were found on the site, together with bones of red deer, boar, birds and other wild fauna. A fragment of a polished flint axe was also found, probably of a pointed-butt type; it was evidently a refined version of an Ertebølle axe. It is not surprising, however, that the hunters of the Ertebølle culture sought new means to support life, for the quantity of available game was decreasing.

Fig. 7. A-beaker.

The evidence for this depopulation can be adduced from the settlement sites of the Ertebølle culture along the fjords and coasts of northern and north-eastern Denmark, settlement sites known as kitchen-middens because of the enormous quantities of refuse, especially oyster shells, which they produce. During the Early Neolithic period the large animals, the elk and aurochs for instance, were almost eradicated by the hunter, and the greatly increased human population had to support itself by fishing and gathering wild fruits—wasteful and difficult ways of obtaining food. The remains of cannibalism in the kitchen-middens seem to suggest a definite lack of food during this period. One of the more sordid and grisly finds which may point to starvation among these people is that from Dyrholmen in East Jutland. Not only had the human long bones found on this site been split for marrow but faint scratches on cervical

Plate 7

vertebrae indicate that decapitation was carried out. The position of the cuts, however, indicates a certain amateurish- ness, for no anatomist, and presumably no life-long cannibal, would have attempted to cut up the human body in such a manner. The head had been scalped with a circular cut of a flint knife, but no such cut would have been necessary to reach the edible brain. The practice of scalping is not only recorded from North America; it is also known from the prehistoric period in South Russia. It seems most probable, however, that it was hunger that occasionally drove the Ertebølle people to cannibalism.

But the shortage of game must not lead us to imagine a com- plete change of life in the settlements along the lakes and coasts; the kitchen-middens demonstrate that hunting and gathering played an important part in the economy of the country.

The natural vegetation of the country that faced the first farmers had changed considerably since the Maglemosean period. The pine forest had given way to a deciduous mixed forest of oak, elm and lime, a change caused by the new, mild, humid Atlantic climate. Dense primeval forest covered the country, crossed only by paths first trodden by game and then used by man. The trees grew close to one another, old ones fell and blocked the path, creepers smothered the trees and linked them with the undergrowth of hazel, juniper and hawthorn, and mistletoe, nowadays practically unknown in Denmark, throve in this exuberance. The bear, wild cat, lynx, wild boar and beaver still lived in the forests but elk and aurochs, the most important game, had become rare. There were, however, plenty of birds by the lakes and along the shore, such as ducks and geese and more exotic birds, as, for example, the great auk, which still survives in the Black Sea area, and the crested pelican, which is now extinct.

The first farmers, then, used small clearings in the forest and collected leaves as cattle fodder, but a complete change in the life of the forest took place with the introduction of the slash-and-burn methods of clearing. This new phase is typified in the archaeological record by the introduction of a new type of pottery vessel with a rounded bottom, high neck and a rim which curves gently outwards (B-pottery). The change in method in forest clearance is seen in the bogs as a layer of charcoal. The first tree to appear after the firing of the forest was the birch, which thrives on ashy soil and open ground, and has a fairly rapid regeneration period; with the birch appear numerous different grasses, amongst which is plantain. Cereal pollen shows that cultivated fields existed alongside the pasture land.

Fig. 8.
B-beaker.

Plate 8

The area of land which had been submitted to the slash-and-burn treatment must have been, as the bogs so clearly show, very extensive and it is also evident that the farmers kept the areas open for their cattle. The method of slash-and-burn is known in many parts of the world. It is used to this day in parts of Finland, where the farmers clear the pine forest by burning and plant their seeds in the ash which fertilizes the soil. It is easier, however, to set fire to a pine forest than to one of leafy, deciduous trees. Recent experiments in South Jutland have illustrated some of the problems that faced Stone Age man. Although the fallen, dry trees probably eased the task of burning the forest in the Neolithic period, a great deal of preparatory work would have to be done in the way of felling trees and cutting down bushes; but it is possible that the amount of work was reduced by cutting through the bark of the trees and allowing them to wither. A heavy, effectively hafted axe was needed for this work, and blades of such axes, thin-butted and polished, are known from innumerable finds all over Denmark. The haft of the axe has survived in occasional bog-finds, from which it is seen that the blade had been placed in a socket wedge-wise,

Plate 9

the thin butt of the axe emerging at the back of the haft. A reconstruction of such an axe has been used recently and proved surprisingly effective—a large tree was felled with it in rather less than an hour. The cutting-edge of such an axe is almost as sharp as steel and does not chip as easily as one might think. It is necessary, however, to sharpen the axe from time to time and many examples show that a new edge has been cut and polished.

When the forest had been burnt, the charred tree-trunks were dragged away, but the stumps were probably left in the ground until they had rotted sufficiently to be easily removed.

The large clearings formed by this method were kept open by grazing cattle and by the removal of the young trees which started to grow after the fire. The primeval forest thus for ever lost its grip on the country.

At Havnelev in South Zealand there is a settlement site which has produced the characteristic pottery of this period together with tools strongly reminiscent of the Late Ertebølle culture, but with some original features. Thin-butted axes are found side by side with flake-axes. The flake and discoidal scrapers, however, are of a quality inferior to those found at typical Ertebølle sites, such as those found at Strandegård in the same area; but local differences of this kind are to be expected. Throughout the entire Neolithic period we find different economies functioning side by side, some communities depend-ing mainly on fishing, some mainly on farming.

From this period of colonization we have a few inhumation graves, in which the bodies of the dead were placed in an oval pit surrounded by pottery vessels, probably containing food. Votive deposits of pottery were still placed in the lakes as an offering to powers who could be influenced by gifts of food.

Plate 12

In the following period (C), the first *dysser* appear and from the same period we have evidence of a village community at Barkær, East Jutland.

Fig. 9

Characteristic of this period is the highly decorated pottery —beakers with flat bottoms and high funnel necks, collared

Plate 13

flasks and lugged amphorae. A great deal of this pottery was found at the settlement site at Barkær which was situated on a small peninsula (about 200 yards across) in a bay in Djursland. Two large rectangular houses were built side by side on this peninsula, separated by a broad road paved in stone, the lake serving as a defensive moat on three sides. One house was about 266 feet long and 20 feet wide, the other slightly shorter. Each house was divided into a series of rooms, about 10 feet in length: the longer contained twenty-six rooms and probably housed twenty-six families. A complete community therefore lived and worked together in these houses. They seem to have been built of wood, the walls and roof being supported by a series of upright posts. The walls of the house and the partitions between each room were probably made of wicker-work and it is reasonable to suppose that a packing material was used, though no traces of clay daub remain on the site.

Trampled into the floor were numerous potsherds, a few polished, thin-butted axes, a number of flint dagger-blades and a sort of pointed halberd, which might possibly be the descen-dant of the Mesolithic pointed weapon. Flat quern-stones were also found and, in a series of small pits, a large number of amber beads and a complete collared flask, offerings to the powers who protected the house and its inhabitants.

The people of this period built the impressive megalithic graves, known as *dysser*, set in a round or oval mound and surrounded by a kerb of stones. The chamber is usually built of flat, massive boulders in the form of a rectangle and roofed

Fig. 9

by a large, closely fitting block of stone. Frequently one of the short sides is lower than the other three, forming a threshold. Very occasionally they were sunk below ground-level. Al-though these first *dysser* are not large, they bear witness to a keen sense of architecture and engineering. The stones forming the wall sloped inwards to prevent their spreading when they took the stress imposed upon them by the large capstone.

When the walls had been erected, the earth mound was thrown up to the height of the top of the chamber; the capstone was then hoisted into position. It is difficult to imagine how Neolithic man with the primitive tackle at his disposal could have manœuvred these stones into position; they may not seem large in the eyes of a modern engineer, but a great deal of ingenuity

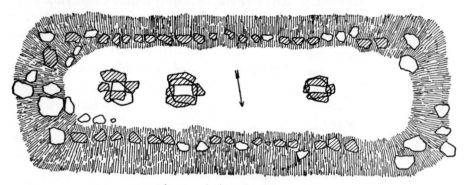

Fig. 9. Long dysse *with three chambers.*

would be needed to hoist them into position without pulleys and cranes. King Frederik VII of Denmark, himself an energetic amateur archaeologist, put forward a theory concerning this problem in a small paper published in the middle of the last century. His theory is probably correct and has been largely confirmed by recent discoveries. The stone was first levered into position on a series of tree-trunks, serving admirably as rollers; as the stone was moved along the ground, the roller which was left free at the back would be moved to the front again. The most difficult part of the operation was to place the stone in position over the chamber: it seems probable that a long ramp was built of earth and wood and the capstone floated on rollers over the top of the chamber to its final position by means of levers and temporary fillings.

The mound is usually some six feet high and is surrounded by a kerb of standing stones: the kerb of the round *dysse* is circular, while that of the long *dysse* is rectangular and often very long. The long *dysse* can contain up to four chambers. Sometimes the *dysser* occur in pairs alongside each other; the most striking example of this is to be seen at Oles Kobbel on the island of Als. The two *dysser* are perfect architectural conceptions, complementing each other and the gently rolling countryside of the neighbourhood. Each *dysse* has stones of the same height, and each has one chamber, yet they are orientated in opposite directions.

An interesting set of grave goods from this period can be seen in Plate 13. Here are the characteristic pottery vessels, the funnel-necked beaker, the amphorae and the collared flask with a stone head mace. The battle-axe which is also known as a 'polygonal axe', has a flat, round butt and an angular, slender body. Another tool occasionally found in this context is the thin-butted, polished flint axe.

Flat inhumation graves are also known from this period. In the simple pits the dead lie, as they did in earlier periods, in a sleeping position surrounded by pottery vessels containing food and drink. Ornaments and other objects were placed in the graves; the woman would take her amber beads with her to the grave and the man his axe, his tool and his weapon of defence. The graves and their contents reflect the busy, uncertain life of the farmer, guarding his property against a multitude of perils, against other farmers and against the hunters of the Late Ertebølle culture who still survived along the coast.

It is perhaps of interest here to turn our attention to this surviving hunter population before continuing the story of the formal Neolithic people. We have already seen how large parts of North Jutland and East Denmark were submerged by the sea for long periods while South-west Denmark rose to a greater height above sea-level. This submergence was responsible for the salt water of the North Sea reaching Zealand. The

Plate 13

oyster, which today only occurs in the shallow waters of the Limfjord, was then found in the bays and inlets of Zealand and the Sound. Oysters were gathered and eaten in large quan/tities by the Ertebølle people, as can be clearly seen from the huge shell mounds, or kitchen/middens. Amongst the litter of oyster shells and discarded tools in these mounds are to be found remains of other shell/fish, such as sea mussels and periwinkles, which with other animal and fish bones must have produced a very distinctive smell!

From the horrible remains of these mounds we can glean certain information about the economy of the people. Carefully carved bone fish/hooks and fishing/nets were used by the Erte/bølle people: a bog/find in Scania, for instance, has produced a fine/meshed net tied to sticks. The fish/spear and leister were not used as commonly as in the Maglemosean period. Among the fish bones are those of deep/sea fish, cod, plaice and dog/fish, which indicate the use of boats (dug/out canoes, perhaps, or kayaks) by the fishermen. Beautifully made dug/out canoes of this period were found at Åmosen.

The seal was an animal much sought after by the hunters of the Late Ertebølle culture. From it came not only meat but bone and skin, and oil for use in the squat, oval, bowl/shaped lamps which are so similar in form to those used by the modern Eskimos of Greenland. The Eskimos use moss as wicks in their lamps, and it is possible that the Ertebølle people used the same material, for greasy fragments of the wick can be seen inside some of the bowls.

Even the whale was hunted for its meat and blubber, for Ertebølle tools have been found in association with the skull of a whale in an East Jutland bay.

The tools of the Ertebølle people are not found solely in the kitchen/middens, they are also found in dark culture layers along the coast and occasionally inland near bogs where dis/carded tools of wood and bone have been preserved. A related culture, descended from the Maglemosean people, is found along the rivers and streams of Jutland.

Fig. 5a

The core-axe of this period is similar to that used by the Early Ertebølle people, but now the edge is often strengthened and sharpened by small, close trimmings, a technique derived from that used on the polished Neolithic axes. The most common axe, the flake-axe, being difficult to manipulate, was perhaps mounted in a heavy wooden haft. One of the main

Fig. 6

material characteristics of the culture, however, is the transverse arrow-head, a descendant of the rhomboid microlith. It may not seem very suitable for its purpose, but it was popular, and one example has been found fastened in a slit at the tip of an arrow and secured by bast.

The quality in flint-work was still high and many of the tools of the earlier culture, borers, scrapers and burins, for example, continued to be made in their original form. Polished axes of soft greenstone were becoming common, but the material from which they were made was unsuitable for hewing wood. The axes are either flat, or they have a pointed oval or a round cross-section, with a broad butt and pecked surface.

Tools of bone and antler continued to be manufactured. Axe-blades were made from antler beams; the haft, which is occasionally found, passed through a sawn-off tine, while the blade was cut obliquely and polished. The bone combs found on sites of this period have an almost modern appearance; they were probably not used exclusively as toilet articles but as tools for carding wool and plant fibres. We have already noticed the bone fish-hooks and the two types of pottery.

The Ertebølle people buried their dead, with some care and reverence, in simple graves in the kitchen-middens themselves. They were buried on their backs with few grave goods (occasionally a bone knife is found in the grave), though stones are sometimes laid along one side of the body or around the head. The high lime content of the shell mounds has often preserved the skeletons in good condition, and we can see from the remains that the people represented in the graves, both those with long heads and those with round heads, would not look at all conspicuous in Denmark today.

The people of Denmark in the *Middle Neolithic period* still led their different lives, groups of varying economic structure living side by side with one another. The Early Neolithic Funnel-Necked Beaker people, both those who buried their dead in *dysser* and those who did not, retained their culture in this period. Influenced from the West, the Megalithic Funnel-Necked Beaker people started to build larger *dysser* and chamber tombs. The Ertebølle people remained in their coastal settlements, with little change in their material life, although they gradually merged with the other groups that flourished in this period. Two new cultures did, however, appear in Denmark at this time: the Single-Grave culture and the Pitted Ware culture.

The development of the culture which produced the large megalithic tombs was stable and continuous, and is of great interest. The two important settlement sites of this people, Troldebjerg on the island of Langeland and Bundsø on the island of Als, not only supply us with information about their houses and material economy but also give us insight into their thoughts and beliefs.

The excavations at Troldebjerg were carried out by an amateur archaeologist, Jens Winther, who found a long rectangular house, more than 200 feet in length, which was divided up, as at Barkær, into a series of small rooms. The roof was carried by a number of posts set, at two metre intervals, in stone-lined sockets. Traces of one of the long walls were found forming a trench in the ground, and from this it could be seen that the walls were made of wicker-work, stretched over a series of vertical posts and daubed with clay. Near the long house were a number of round huts, and hearths were found both inside and outside the houses. From a pit under the floor of the long house came the most remarkable find from the site, a complete pot and an axe with its cutting-edge upwards. This may be interpreted as a symbol of the power of the axe, and as an offering to a power greater even than the axe. From such deposits and offerings of axes, sometimes under strange conditions, on other, later sites, we can catch a glimpse of prehistoric man's religion.

The Troldebjerg settlement is situated on a slope which ran down towards a lake, a situation ideal both for hunting and fishing as well as for farming. But the settlement site at Bundsø gives a better idea of the economy of these people. Although no houses survived here the artifacts are typical of the Middle Neolithic period, consisting of polished or unpolished thick-butted flint axes, chisels, scrapers of a characteristic round shape and fragments of a fine ornamented pottery. The quality of flint-flaking is clumsy. One type of flake, which was sometimes trimmed along the back, was probably used as a simple unhafted sickle, a bunch of ears being gathered in one hand and cut with the flint held in the other. The grain grown by these people can be studied either in a carbonized condition or from the impression left in the pottery, where grain has accidentally been mixed into the clay before firing. Fragments of food, probably made from flour, have been found in certain vessels; similar left-overs are known from other periods (and especially from the Iron Age) but are usually too greatly decomposed for identification.

The commonest cultivated cereals were the primitive varieties of wheat, einkorn and emmer, but naked barley was also found; whereas on other sites from the same period the latter is the commonest variety. Dwarf wheat and common wheat were occasionally found. To these nourishing foods the housewife added seeds of plants, goose-foot for instance. Raspberries and apples were gathered from bushes and trees. Two types of apple were available, the small crab-apple and, planted near the house, a larger apple, grown from imported trees, of a variety known in the settlement sites near the Swiss lakes.

The Bundsø people kept live-stock, mainly pigs, but some cattle. The large pig population indicates a predominating forest vegetation, which could produce acorn and other pig-food. These animals differ distinctly from the wild varieties, and there can be no doubt that they are imported stock, and not a recently domesticated wild type. Sheep are not quite as common as pigs, but as they demand open grazing land, they demonstrate the fact that the Bundsø people cleared large areas of the forest, an operation in which the sheep themselves took part by eating the young shoots. The sheep of the European Stone, Bronze and Iron Ages were rather different from modern sheep, their most noticeable feature being their large goat-like horns. A few goats were kept, but only as dairy animals; sheep, providing wool, meat and clothing in greater quantities, were obviously more profitable.

Although more than one hundred thousand domesticated animal bones were found at Bundsø, a mere hundred and fifty of wild animals, representing only a few varieties—red deer, wild boar and aurochs—were found. Such figures demonstrate the complete change in economy from hunting to farming. The same trend is illustrated by the remains of dog found on the site; the large hunting-dog of the Early Stone Age was gradually replaced by a smaller watch-dog and new breeds of dogs were introduced.

These people of the Middle Neolithic period not only built larger *dysser* than those constructed in the Early Neolithic period, they also introduced a new type of tomb: the passage-grave. Both these tomb types have an entrance to the chamber which allows for continued use, and it can be seen from the skeletal remains, in certain passage-graves especially, that many generations of the dead were buried here. The large *dysser*

Plates 10 and 11

47

with their bold profile became a prominent feature of the Danish landscape, receiving individual names at an early stage of the country's history. They are only found in certain areas of Denmark, as, for example, Als, North-west Zealand and East Jutland, where they are especially common. Most impressive, perhaps, is the round *dysse*, Påskær stenhus, at Knebel, north-east of Århus, surrounded by its ring of massive boulders. The long *dysser*, biggest in Blommeskobbel, near Mom-mark on the island of Als, are also beautifully constructed monuments. The stones used in tomb construction in this period are much larger than those used in the Early Neolithic period. The builders of these tombs were skilled, brave men; they juggled with the stones as though fighting enormous beasts of prey. With the instinct of engineers they judged the shape and centre of gravity of a stone which, if it was not handled carefully, could crush a man to death in the twinkling of an eye. It must have been a great and important moment when the huge capstone was finally hoisted into position on the gently sloping walls. The chamber was high—a man could easily stand upright in it—and was often pentagonal in shape; the entrance was narrow and a low transverse stone formed a threshold. The chamber was covered by a mound.

Plates 19 and 20

The passage-graves have oval or rectangular chambers and very occasionally examples with connecting chambers or with two chambers placed side by side are found. The chamber is barely as high as a man and is entered on one long side by a low passage through which one has to crawl on hands and knees. The thresholds of stone probably used to carry wooden doors. The tombs are impressive pieces of architecture with walls of enormous flat stones placed side by side and sloping slightly inwards to take the weight of the capstone, the spaces between the stones being filled with dry stone walling. These large stones formed an artificial cave dimly lit through the passage, emphasizing the difference between the ancestral house of the dead and the house of the living. The passage-graves and the *dysser* were built by the same people who built the long houses. At a site which is still being excavated at Tustrup, north-east of Århus, two *dysser*, one passage-grave and the remains of an uninhabited building are being investigated. The latter was rectangular with three walls built of heavy stone, the fourth side was open. The outside faces of the walls were covered by stone slabs placed on end, as was the inside face of the short side wall. The other two had been lined with a vertical timber construction laid on a sleeper foundation.

Plate 17

There was no hearth in this solid, rather low house, but two isolated groups of potsherds were found on the floor. The sherds represent thirty well-made, decorated pottery vessels, the commonest type being the pedestal bowls (known as fruit bowls) and a series of ladles, both well-known types in the passage-graves. The pedestal bowls formed a set with the clay ladles and were perhaps used for pouring out libations for the dead. That this house is not a dwelling is certain, but it is not easy to ascertain its proper function.

Plate 14

The chamber of the two megaliths excavated at Tustrup have long since been robbed, a circumstance which does not unduly disturb the Danish archaeologist, as it has been repeatedly shown that rich finds can be made outside the tombs, usually in the forecourt. This proved to be the case here. A collection of sherds was scattered outside the tombs and we may assume that pots were placed here and that they contained food for the dead, who were perhaps thought to live on inside the grave. But we will return to the subject of the survival of the dead when we discuss the burial customs of the Iron Age and its strange cult of the dead.

The excavation of a passage-grave known as Grønhøj (the Green Barrow) at Horsens in the east of Jutland has revealed unusually interesting information about these offerings to the dead. More than a hundred years ago Worsaae started to

Fig. 10

excavate this passage-grave, as one of his first experiments in archaeology. The experiment was not very successful, however, for one of the large capstones in the chamber collapsed and consequently the excavation was abandoned. In 1940 modern archaeologists started to investigate this site again.

Grønhøj has a small oval chamber, in which two levels of inhumation burials with tools and vessels were found undisturbed. The lower layer can be dated to the period of the building of the tomb, and the upper layer to the end of the Stone Age.

Outside the passage, close to the stones of the kerb, about seven thousand potsherds and a number of upturned pots were found. The excavator turned his attention to the tall stones of the kerb, and found on them sherds of pottery which could be joined to the sherds from the area outside the kerb. The solution to the problem thus became clear. The pots were originally placed on or behind the kerb, perhaps filled with food and drink as an offering to the dead. Many thousands of potsherds could be joined together to form vessels and ladles belonging to the same period as those found in the bottom layer of the chamber. The evidence provided by the finds from this site has proved conclusively that the old theory, that the potsherds found outside megalithic tombs are the result of a periodic clearance of the chamber, is not always correct.

Against this background of votive offerings, the strange stone-built house at Tustrup is perhaps explicable. The house was used for only a short time before it was destroyed by fire— presumably intentionally. The excavator believes that the initial offerings were made here before the tomb was completed.

The material finds, both from graves and settlement sites, show a continuous development from a starting-point in the Early Neolithic period. This development is especially evident in the sequence of ornament and form of the pottery; the ornaments incised in the walls of the vessels are filled with chalk

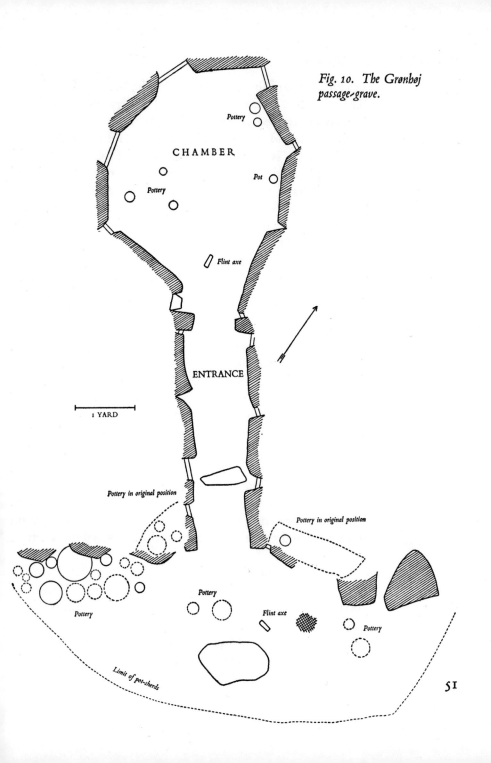

Fig. 10. The Grønhøj
passage-grave.

Pottery

CHAMBER

Pot

Pottery

Flint axe

ENTRANCE

1 YARD

Pottery in original position

Pottery in original position

Pottery

Pottery

Flint axe

Pottery

Limit of pot-sherds

51

producing a striking contrast against the brown of the fabric. The ornament of the earliest type of pottery in this period is formed of reserved zigzag bands and impressions of twisted cord. It is found on the Trollebjerg site and in its most pronounced form is known as 'the grand style'. Coeval with the grand style is 'the refined style' one of the most graceful and elegant styles of pottery decoration of the prehistoric period. The tools used for the decoration were very simple but carefully chosen, the edge of a cardial shell or a small bone comb being the most common. Later on in this period there is a marked decrease in taste and sense of form: the ornamentation begins to take the form of imitation twisted cord decoration, while later still it is formed of large V-shaped motifs.

The ornamentation of pottery of this period was developed locally, but occasional glimpses of intrusive influences can be traced, especially from Central Germany and Western Europe. The odd vessel with stylized face is evidence of contact with the latter area and emphasizes the connections between the megalithic graves of Denmark and those of Western Europe.

At a time when the passage-graves were still being used, but well into the Middle Neolithic period, a new culture (or rather three related cultural groups) appears in the country, known as the Battle-Axe or, as opposed to the megalithic cultures, the Single-Grave culture. There is no material connection between the Single-Grave and the megalithic cultures, and its advent in Denmark must be interpreted as an immigration from areas in the south and east where its material finds can be paralleled.

Finds of this culture have been recovered from low barrows, often found near streams and pastures in the sandy interior of Jutland. By the end of the last century it had become obvious, through excavation, that these mounds had grown over a period of years, as one burial was placed on top of the other, each barrow representing a sequence of several generations. In

Plate 15, left

Plate 24

Plate 21

a typical barrow the first grave is cut into the ground and the body laid on its side in a sleeping position with an ordinary axe and a battle-axe (or, in the case of a woman, amber beads) and occasionally a pot presumably filled with food. The next body was placed on top of the first grave in a similar position and a low barrow raised over it. This sequence continued and the barrow gradually grew in size. The practice must have been popular, for it sometimes continued well into the Late Neo-lithic period. In Plate 23 a sequence of three characteristic grave-groups of the Single-Grave people is illustrated, the earliest being that on the left. The beaker of this early stage has a conical neck and a rounded body with horizontal cord-impressions under the rim. Close parallels of this pottery are found in Saxo-Thuringia, and it seems probable that the Battle-Axe people spread from this area as far north as the Limfjord in Jutland.

Plate 22

Plate 23

A second stage is represented by the gently curved beaker with incised decoration, and the final stage by a small flower-pot-like vessel (Plate 15, right, and Plate 23).

From the many hundreds of graves of this culture which have been excavated a large amount of material has been collected which allows both chronological and geographical division. The classification of this material by Professor Glob has been very detailed; the various forms of the greenstone axe, starting from the simple robust forms with drooping cutting-edge and developing later into slender, elegant objects, are particularly suited for such division.

The distribution of the single-graves shows that these people were not primarily farmers but stock-breeders whose cattle grazed along the streams and in the open plains.

Rather late in the Middle Neolithic period we find a related group of people in East Jutland and the islands. Their beakers are not unlike that illustrated in Plate 23, centre; that is, a curved, rather wide vessel with a large zigzag pattern. They have left their traces in a number of graves and in a few U-shaped huts.

A third group, connected with East Scandinavia, is known from Bornholm and the other islands in the east of Denmark. It is known as the Boat-Axe culture, taking its name from the boat-like profile of its short-socketed axes. Occasionally these polished greenstone axes are found in stone cists with a heavy polished flint gouge. The characteristic pots of this culture are of oval profile and are covered with linear ornament or with comb-impressions.

Yet another culture of this period is the Pitted Ware culture named after its characteristic pottery, which is decorated with a series of deeply-punched holes. The vessels have a short, wide neck, tailing away to an almost pointed base and decorated with impressed chevrons and triangles as well as the typical pits. The culture is first recognized in the Scandinavian peninsula, but extended to the eastern seaboard of Denmark. The material recovered from both settlements and inhumation burials demon-strates that, although the Pitted Ware people kept pigs, their economy was based primarily on hunting. The most charac-teristic tools are fish-hooks and long triangular arrow-heads, but harpoons and spear-heads with rilled edges also occur, as do strange triangular plaques of bone. One of the commonest and most typical objects found on Pitted Ware sites is the cylindrical flint core from which flakes were struck.

All these different cultural groups could not be expected to live together without a certain amount of friction. Even within the groups themselves peace could not always be maintained; cattle-rustling, for instance, must have flourished in any primitive stock-breeding community. The presence of the beautifully polished greenstone battle-axes in the men's graves indicates something of this lack of security, for the battle-axes were obviously weapons. Whether the weapon be the elegant double-axe from the passage-graves, the efficient battle-axe

from the single-graves or the boat-axe from the East, the story
is the same and is further illustrated by grim finds from the
burials. Many skulls in the megalithic graves show deep cuts
in the forehead or temple and deep blows, as from a heavy club,
at the back of the head. Arrow-heads are found in collar-bones
Plate 18
and one grave has produced a skull which has been pierced
from above, through the nose, by an arrow. All these tell stories
of wars and quarrels long before written history. The world of
those who finally found a resting-place in the great stone tombs
was neither secure nor peaceful. But the wounded did not
always die untended; surgeons carried out competent operations
with their flint tools, and although some patients died, some
survived. Broken bones, for instance, were often set with such
skill that the patient must have recovered so completely as to
walk without a limp.

The strangest operation of all carried out by the surgeons of
this period was trepanning. This practice had nothing, perhaps,
to do with healing wounds; it may merely have been carried
out in order to relieve a headache or as some sort of religious
rite. Skulls are found from which round plaques have been cut
with a sharp flint knife; whether the patient was conscious or
not during this daring operation is not known, but despite the
Plate 16
rough treatment the subjects must have received they sometimes survived and lived.

But not all contacts between the different groups were
hostile: there is plenty of evidence of trade. Ingots of high-
quality flint, some of it mined, were a valuable commodity, as
was salt and the attractive amber which could be collected
along the shore. These were but some of the materials that were
traded throughout the Scandinavian area and beyond it.
Among the many other materials that were traded in this
period was copper, which later became so important as an alloy
of bronze. It first appears in the period of the early *dysser* in
the form of beads and small plaques; later on, an increasing

number of copper tools and weapons appear. One of the most important finds in this connection is that from Bygholm, which produced a number of copper axes and a dagger with a large piece of pottery of Early Passage-Grave type.

A number of crescentic gold collars, known as lunulae, have been related to similar Irish ornaments and, although they are not imports, they indicate some sort of cultural contact with the British Isles.

The *Late Neolithic period* is one of change. The dead were most commonly buried in large stone cists, although the *dysser*, passage-graves and single-graves were still in use. The battle-axe disappears, to be replaced by the dagger, beautifully made after the manner of the period, of flint precisely trimmed by flat flaking. Behind the flint weapon one can see its metal prototype, for the flint-smith had imitated the fish-tail pommel of the bronze daggers known elsewhere in Europe. The flint technique of this period is of incomparable quality and is nowhere better seen than on the daggers, the surface of which was polished before the final trimming. The smith knew the virtues and limitations of his material and exploited them to their full extent, using even the colour of the flint to aid the elegance of his workmanship, as can be seen from the dagger from Hindsgavl with its warm nuances of brown and blue. Here the flint-craftsman reached the zenith of his achievement.

We see the same quality of work in the arrow-heads: where in the earlier period these were simple pointed flakes, now they are the triumph of a craftsman's art, heart-shaped and barbed. These arrows, with other innovations of the period, reached Denmark from Western and Central Europe. Such innovations include the use of bronze and the introduction of simple pottery. One of the characteristic tools of this period is the flat bronze axe. This appears in two forms: the first, with a wide curved blade, comes from Central Europe; the other, with faceted edges and occasional incised decorations, from the West.

Plate 26

Plate 25

A characteristic of all these axes is the wide, rounded cuttingedge that was accidentally formed during the manufacture of the axe, for the edge was hammered sharp and the metal spread out in this fashion towards the sides.

With the Late Neolithic period we become involved in the introduction of metal and the early stages of the Bronze Age, and to this we must now turn our attention.

CHAPTER IV

The Bronze Age

ALTHOUGH THERE IS NO BASIC difference between the Late Neolithic and the Early Bronze Age, the intro-duction of the art of bronze-casting was epoch making. In this period the social structure of the community stands out with a greater clarity than ever before. It is astonishing that craftsmen, with no tradition in the arts of the metalworker and with no local sources either of copper or tin, should have acquired in such a very short time a skill comparable with that of their fellow-craftsmen in countries more richly endowed with the raw materials of their art. It is even more astonishing that the quality of the workmanship and decoration of the Scandinavian bronze-smith is often at least as high as that found in any other European country. Opportunities for such a demon-stration of the craftsman's skill could only occur in conjunction with the acquisition of wealth based on active trade. Whether or not the smiths actually learnt their trade outside the country, we do not know for certain; but it is clear that without direct training they would not have been able to master their new and difficult art. The trade which supported their art must have been based on efficient transport, on roomy boats and wagons, or at least on pack-horses, and we must consider these factors in conjunction with the art of the bronze-smith.

The raw materials of the bronze-smith's craft had to be imported as ingots over great distances. Copper was mined in many parts of Western and Central Europe but tin was a rarer commodity, mined in only a few places in Europe in the pre-historic era. The best-known tin-mining area in Western Europe in this period was Cornwall and we know that in Roman times Cornish tin was imported into the Mediterranean area along the rivers of France.

The copper-mines in Mitterberg, Austria, demonstrate the mining techniques of the period: tunnels were made by first heating the rock with fire and then pouring cold water over the warmed area. The stone cracked and was further crushed by hammers and carried out from the tunnels in baskets. The passage was shored up with timber and care was taken in the provision of ventilation. The mines were situated in a forested area, so wood was available in large quantities for the fire that was used to separate the metal from the ore.

Tin generally occurs in nature in a crystalline form and it is remarkable that man, at this early stage, had already discovered the complicated process necessary for the extraction of the metal. It is even more remarkable that he had discovered the use of tin in conjunction with copper, in the proportions of 1:9, to produce bronze. This discovery was not, however, made in Europe but in the Middle East, whence the knowledge of agriculture had spread long before. Soon the metal-using people of the Near East turned their attention to Europe, which was a source of ore and a market for their finished goods. The knowledge of bronze-casting spread northwards and by about 1500 B.C. had reached the areas to the south of Denmark.

Plate 28

At this period the first shining bronze objects appeared in Denmark, and in defiance of these new marvels the flint crafts-men were spurred on to produce incredibly elaborate imitations. The flint-smith copied the new bronze daggers and axes in the old medium—he even copied the single- and double-edged sword; but it was all in vain. His exquisite craftsmanship was wasted; for who would now appreciate the brittle but beautiful flint tools when faced with strong, serviceable objects of bright metal? Craftsmen of the younger generation were apprenticed to foreign smiths and learnt from them the new art. Soon we meet bronze objects of Scandinavian character, of the highest quality, and it is with these objects that the Bronze Age of Denmark really begins.

Plate 26

The first bronze artifacts produced in Denmark were simple flat-axes and daggers, contemporary with similar British types and types from the Central European Unětice culture. These axes, which are found together with imported objects, are unmistakably of local manufacture; the material from which they are made is a bronze, containing very little tin.

In the ensuing period the smiths gained complete mastery of their material and the objects from Valsømagle, Zealand, which show marked Scandinavian characteristics, ably demonstrate this. The find consists of a sword (Plate 27, second from the left), four spear-heads (one is illustrated in Plate 35, bottom), three axes (for use as weapons), a palstave (a narrow-bladed axe with high flanges on either side) and a fish-hook. This find is probably not a grave-group but a hoard, buried maybe by a smith. The craftsman who made these objects was a master of his art; they bear witness to his sensitive and rather eclectic taste. His interest in fishing is not only evident from the fish-hook but also from the little shoal of fish which decorates the socket of the spear. Another motif on this socket is the double spiral which is well known in the period of the shaft-graves of Greece (*c.* 1500 B.C.) and which passed northwards through Hungary to Denmark, where this simple, rather playful, design is handled with virtuosity and imagination. The motif demands careful execution and the Valsø spear-head shows how, even at this early stage, it was handled with skill and sensitivity to bring out the qualities of light and shade on the shiny surface of the metal.

The axes from this find have a horizontal rib along their sides but are otherwise similar to more robust specimens, one of which is illustrated in Plate 35, centre. This axe has a fine geometrical pattern, giving a tattooed effect on the smooth skin of the bronze. The palstave was developed from the flanged flat-axe with expanded cutting-edge. Hafted palstaves found in tree-trunk coffins show that the haft was formed from a heavy

Plate 27

Plate 35

Plate 35

branch with a lateral branch at an acute angle. The lateral branch was cut off the tree at a suitable length and the end was split to take the narrow butt of the palstave. Halfway down the blade was a ridge which acted as a stop to prevent the haft splitting.

The sword from the find is beautifully made with a carefully fashioned hilt. It was a thrusting sword (or rapier) and the hilt is so small that it can only have accommodated three fingers of the hand, the other two must have curled behind the knob. Slashing swords are rare in this period, but a recently discovered example—a curved sword, in beautiful condition (Plate 26, centre)—was found in a bog in West Zealand. It is a heavy weapon, relying on its weight rather than on its cutting edge; the curved end is thick and weighted by three bosses and it is decorated in a similar manner to the axe illustrated in the centre of Plate 35. The distinctive shape of this sword is ultimately derived from the slashing swords of the Near East.

Plate 26

We can suppose that similar swords were manufactured in Eastern and Central Europe, but few examples survive and it is evident that the thrusting sword was of more common occurrence. A few thrusting swords were imported into Denmark, and one such—a beautiful Hungarian example—is illustrated in Plate 27, bottom left.

Plate 28

The following period (Period II), which covers the last part of the second millennium B.C., is represented by numerous grave mounds. Many of the large barrows, so common in the Danish countryside, were built during this period, but there is far more to these monuments than a hump on the skyline. These mounds reflect the society that built them. Excavations in them hint at the amount of work and capital necessary for their construction. The barrows were made of stones and enormous quantities of turf; indeed, whole fields must have been stripped of their turf and a considerable amount of grazing land sacrificed, to make a barrow 9 feet high and 60 feet across. The body was buried in a stone cist or in a coffin made from a hollowed tree-trunk provided with a handle at either end to make carrying easier. The cist or coffin was covered by a heap of stones and capped by turf. Such work could only be undertaken for the burial of a rich man, the poor could not expect such a grand send-off.

Plate 30

Plate 29

The burials are placed on the tops of hills looking out over a wide area and the mounds can be seen for many miles. Often they were built in rows and Sophus Müller was the first to suggest that this phenomenon is due to the fact that the barrows lay along the side of a trackway. Such a position is paralleled, for instance, outside Rome, where grave-stones are strung out along the roads that lead from the town, their inscriptions reminding the passers-by of the dead who must not be forgotten. Bound up with this was the old idea of the house of the dead, who lived on inside the grave. Such an idea was prevalent in the Roman Empire and houses were built for the souls of the dead.

Similarly, houses for the dead were built in Northern Europe during the Bronze Age. Best preserved are those in the barrows of Thuringia where they were covered by an earth mound. In other places the houses were burnt down, and occasionally they seem to have served as funeral pyres. Whereas traces of such buildings as occur in Denmark are few and insignificant, well-preserved examples have been discovered just to the south of the border.

The area surrounding the barrow was sometimes enclosed by large stones or wooden posts and it may be assumed that certain ceremonies took place here which have left little trace in the archaeological record. In many cases the marks of plough-shares have been discovered underneath the barrow. This does not necessarily mean that the barrow was built on a ploughed field; a recent find suggests that the ploughing formed part of the ritual of burial.

The continuing importance of the barrow to those who lived in the neighbourhood is indicated by the fact that it often contains several burials, deposited after the barrow had been completed. The first burial is often an inhumation in the centre of the mound; later, cremated bones were placed in pots or simple holes in the sides of the barrow. In this manner the barrows became the dwelling-places and spiritual homes of the dead. Only during the last few hundred years has it been the practice to open these venerable and awe-inspiring tombs, which by now had almost lost their erstwhile significance. A study of the Icelandic sagas and Danish folk-lore gives us an insight into the power represented by those who dwelt in the barrows.

The grave goods buried with the dead indicate that Bronze Age man believed that life continued after death and that certain needs and obligations had to be fulfilled by the living in order to provide for his existence in the barrow. There was a sense of continuity between life and death and no expense was spared to see that the dead person was provided with objects and materials which he would need in the after-life. The wealthy woman was given her ornaments of gold and bronze and the man's weapons were laid beside him in the grave. But there were occasions when a miserly relative placed a simple dagger in a scabbard instead of the long sword: a not very reverent, if human, trait discovered during the excavation of an oak coffin in Jutland. These graves have preserved almost complete outfits of grave goods, such as clothes, wood and metal objects and even the ox-hide which had served as a shroud.

Plate 31

The preservation of so many organic substances is due to a fortunate combination of circumstances. Firstly, the oak coffin was placed on a clay sub-soil which prevented moisture from draining away and thus rotting the cloth, etc.; secondly, the grave was often completely sealed by layers of a certain iron compound which formed a hard crust over the coffin. Lastly, the acid in the oak coffin has excellent preservative properties.

Plate 32

An interesting example of a burial of this character was excavated at Egtved, East Jutland in 1921. Orientated east-west in the bottom of the barrow was an oak coffin. This was taken to the laboratory of the National Museum of Copenhagen and when the lid was lifted a sprig of flowering yarrow was found lying on the ox-hide shroud—a parting gift perhaps, or just placed there by chance? In its quiet, insignificant way it tells us that the burial took place in the summer.

Plate 33, right

Wrapped in the hide was the body of a young woman 5 feet 2½ inches tall and between eighteen and twenty years of age. The bones have disappeared, but the skin, the nails and the enamel of her teeth are preserved. She was dressed in a jacket, with elbow-length sleeves, a short skirt of cords joined together at waist and hem and, round the waist, a belt with intricately worked tassels and a horn comb tucked into it. On the stomach was a round bronze disc with a central spike. Worn thus, it would emphasize, in a charming way, the attraction of the light costume she wore, while at the same time, perhaps, serving to deter the man who admired it from inspecting it too closely! Round each wrist she wore a bronze bracelet.

The young woman was not buried alone, nor was she left without tools or food. Near her head was a box, made of birch-bark, which contained a woollen cord and an awl. The cord can hardly have been meant for sewing as it was tied into a number of knots; perhaps it was a hair-ribbon. Near her feet, on top of the hide, was placed a small birch-bark pail sewn together with bast. Analysis of the dregs revealed that it had contained either beer or a fruit wine. Beneath the hide were found the cremated bones of a six- or seven-year-old child. The riddle of the burial, a riddle that cannot be answered, is—why was the child cremated and the young woman not? Was the child perhaps placed in the grave as a sacrifice?

Another charming representative of the Danish Bronze Age is the young woman whose body was found at Skrydstrup in South Jutland in 1935. The coffin was badly damaged and had to be encased in plaster before being moved to the labora- tory. When the body was uncovered it was found to be sur- prisingly well preserved; the skeleton was intact although the soft parts of the body were slightly shrunken. The body was that of a slender young woman between eighteen and nineteen years of age, 5 feet $6\frac{1}{2}$ inches tall, with a long head and narrow face and blond hair set in an elaborate *coiffure*. She had fine features, long eye-lashes and perfect white teeth; by her ears were two large spirals of thin gold wire and the hair was covered by a net and a beautifully-made cap, tied undeneath the chin, by two long ribbons. Her jacket was similar to that of the Egtved woman and had an embroidered pattern across the sleeves. The body was wrapped in a long piece of cloth, secured round the waist with a belt; although this resembles a skirt, it was probably merely a winding-sheet. The feet were wrapped in small pieces of cloth; nevertheless, we may assume that she, and other people of the Bronze Age, wore leather shoes of a moccasin-like form known from later finds. A chervil at the bottom of the coffin shows that the Skrydstrup woman was also buried during the summer.

Plate 31

Another important find is that from Borum Eshøj, in East Jutland. The woman found in this grave was buried in clothes similar to those of the Skrydstrup woman, and the same barrow contained men's clothes. Sets of men's clothes were also found at Trindhøj in East Jutland and at Muldbjerg in West Jutland. In all these cases the dress consisted of a gown or loin-cloth, a cloak and a round cap. Trousers were not introduced until later, probably through the influence of the eastern nomads.

The Muldbjerg man was dressed in a gown, which was wrapped round the body underneath the arms, while a corner of it was thrown over the shoulder and fastened behind. Round

Plate 33, left

the waist was a belt secured by a bronze hook and a sword was carried in a shoulder-strap. Over the shoulders was a cloak, which reached down below the knees. The dress, like that of the Egtved girl, was light and cool, suitable for the mild summer climate; we may assume that the man wore more substantial clothing during the winter. The clothes were fastened with bronze brooches of a type that will be discussed below.

The man's hemispherical cap is a magnificent piece of work; its texture is somewhat similar to that of a modern bath-towel save that, despite the coarse needles of the period, the small loops are closer together and of finer quality. This is but one example of the amazing skill of these people whose tools were often of the crudest. The cloth used is mainly woven from wool, although occasionally the fibres of plants were used. The wool was first carded, perhaps on a piece of wood covered with thistles, and then spun and twisted into a strong thread on a distaff. It is perhaps strange that no spindle-whorls are known from this period but we know from the Iron Age examples— for instance, one found with the strange boat at Hjortspring on the island of Als—that the spindle may have consisted simply of a stick one end of which was thicker than the other.

The loom on which the cloth was woven has left few archaeological traces, but with the aid of the few loom-weights that have been found it is possible to reconstruct it. The loom-weights, which have a central hole and a lentoid cross-section, are similar to those on a type of vertical loom used in North Scandinavia, the Faroes and Iceland as late as the eighteenth century A.D. The continuity of the tradition of this type of loom is emphasized by finds from Iron Age houses. The loom consisted of two vertical posts bearing a horizontal roller round which the finished cloth was wound. The loom-weights were tied to the vertical threads (the warp) in such a way that the alternate threads could be moved backwards and forwards as the weaving progressed; the weft was beaten into place by a

Plate 62

weaving-sword, a bone example of which has been found with a hilt similar to that of a tanged sword.

Other noteworthy finds from the oak coffins are swords and daggers, some still in their wooden scabbards complete with carved ornaments. A hafted palstave was also found, the haft consisting of a shaft terminating in a lateral branch set at an acute angle. The palstave had been fitted into the split end of this lateral branch. While the design of the pottery of this period is rather indifferent, beautiful boxes of wood and bark have been preserved. For instance, there is a wooden bowl decorated with small tin nails which was found together with a horn spoon and a drinking-horn.

A collapsible fald-stool (a folding stool rather like a modern camp-stool) was found in one of the coffins, consisting of two frames, pivoted in the centre, with wooden runners at top and bottom; the topmost runners have grooves and holes which carried the leather seat. Copies of this chair demonstrate that it must have been most comfortable and it had, of course, the additional virtue of being easily portable. Cylindrical bronze mounts from the frames of such chairs are a fairly common find in the graves of the period.

The chair was a well-designed piece of furniture of a familiar shape, which must have been imported from the South. The type is common in the Near East, especially in Egypt, but is also known in Crete and it was probably from this area that the design reached Denmark.

The sun-chariot from Trundholm, in North-west Zealand, is one of the most impressive finds from the whole of Danish prehistory. It belongs to this period and consists of a large disc, gold-plated on at least one side, carried on six wheels and drawn by a bronze horse; the centre of the disc is decorated (on both sides) with a series of circle and spiral patterns. At the edge of the disc is a loop which corresponds to a loop on the horse's breast and we may assume that the two were connected

Plate 36

by a cord or chain. There is a hole through the horse's mouth which probably carried a bit.

The horse is modelled in the round and when we consider that such a treatment is without parallel in this period and is based on no tradition, we realize what an amazingly fine piece of workmanship it represents. The rounded body with its slender legs and the smooth features of the face show how well the craftsman knew and admired the subject of his art. The animal's neck is decorated with a series of fine lines representing the mane and the protruding eyes are encircled by a star-like motif.

This object with its horse and disc carried on wheels is not easily interpreted, but it seems likely that it represents the sun rather than the moon. Sun-worship is known the world over and it is possible that the people of this period believed that the sun was drawn across the sky by a horse.

The Trundholm find could be assumed to be a model of a larger disc drawn by a live horse; but in that case it would be difficult to explain why the wheels are placed under the horse as well as the disc. It seems most likely, therefore, that we have here a representation of the sun, and of the horse which in the minds of the people is inseparable from it, and that the whole is the object of a cult. But all this is no more than guesswork and we have no real knowledge of the thoughts or beliefs that inspired the creation of this unusual work of art. In the absence of written sources the interpretation of this object's meaning presents overwhelming difficulties and we must face the fact that we cannot, at the present stage of our knowledge, under-stand the religious ideas and beliefs of the Bronze Age. With these reservations, it might be possible to hazard a guess that the Trundholm equipage was used to invoke the life-giving warmth of the sun, which was treated as a god.

The fact that many objects, including the Trundholm sun-chariot, were found in a bog may have some religious signifi-cance. Not far from Trundholm, for instance, six beautiful swords were found in similar terrain. But these bog-finds need not necessarily be taken as votive or sacrificial offerings. In a bog at Smørumovre, near Copenhagen, a hundred and sixty-three bronze objects were found, including sixty spear-heads and eighty-eight axes, several of these objects had come straight from the mould and had not even been properly finished. We must interpret this hoard as the property of a wealthy trader or bronze-founder who had sunk the bronzes in the bog in time of emergency and was presumably unable to reclaim them.

Imported objects are found side by side with locally manu-factured objects during this period, as we have seen also in the early part of the Bronze Age. Among the many imported types is a sword with an octagonal hilt which came from Central Europe. But not all swords of this type were imported; some of them may have been copied and adapted by the bronze-smiths of Scandinavia, as some of the designs have no parallels on the Continent.

The third period of the Bronze Age, which occupied the early part of the first millennium B.C., is characterized by a more tenuous and graceful decoration of the weapons and of the ornaments. The slender hilt of the sword was decorated with an openwork design which was inlaid with some other material to contrast with the shining metal. Another feature is the small Plate 27, right
indentation at the top of the blade where the thumb rested. Tanged swords, the hilts of which consisted of wood, bone or some other perishable material, are also known. The scabbards which held these swords are of especial interest, as they em-phasize the care and attention lavished on the weapon; they consist of thin wooden strips lined with fur and covered with leather.

The most common ornament of this period is the bronze brooch, which acted as a dress fastener, and which had already appeared in the previous period. Its design is based on the

Plate 34

principle of the safety-pin and, although at this stage there was no spiral spring (which first appeared in the Iron Age), it was almost as effective as the later versions. The first Danish brooches of this type were based on a Central European design and were rather clumsy, but in the third period they improve and the bow, which is elegantly ribbed, terminates at both ends in a spiral. The pin is attached to one of the spirals and is closed on a catch attached to the other spiral.

Another popular object was the belt-box, which, like the brooch, underwent characteristic changes during the ensuing periods. It first appears as a small round box with a decorated flat bottom and a flat plain lid with a loop in the centre which corresponded to two loops on the rim. The belt on which it was hung was threaded through the three loops and the lid

Plate 38

was thus secured. It was probably used to carry toilet articles and may be considered as the Bronze Age counterpart of the modern handbag. There is reason to suppose that the bronze belt-box imitates a wooden prototype.

Other portable objects belonging to this period are the arm-rings or bracelets (which were sometimes made of gold), buttons and knives.

The graves still furnish us with important information. The dead were usually buried in a wooden coffin or a stone cist, as in the previous period. Of the many barrow burials of this period, that found at Kivik in South Sweden (in the once Danish province of Scania) is probably the most important. It was opened in 1748 and an unusually large cist (measuring 12 feet by 3 feet), built of stone slabs, was found. The inside face of each slab was decorated with strange carvings; some of them, like the man in a two-wheeled chariot drawn by two horses, are easy to understand; others, like the figures with an S-shaped profile clothed in strange garments, cannot be inter-preted with any certainty and one may only guess that they represent the dead. Other motifs on the stones consist of an *omega* sign and a strange composite design consisting of three-quarters of a circle in which stand two men holding the disc terminals of an inverted anchor-like ornament. It is obvious that these scenes have a definite significance, but it is no longer possible for us to understand their meaning. We can, however, be certain that the Kivik grave was built for an important man.

Still, the graves of the rich are not the only burials that are found during this period; poor graves are also found and the combination of the two emphasize a social structure with a definite class distinction.

At this period cremation was introduced and gradually grew in popularity until, in the Late Bronze Age, it became the prevailing burial custom. The differing customs do not seem to reflect any marked antagonism; rather, the change must be considered as reflecting an alteration in man's ideas concerning the life of the dead. We have already seen an early example of cremation in the Egtved coffin.

A strange but common transitional form between the two rites is provided by the burial of burnt bones within a full-sized stone cist. The grave from Hvidegården, Lyngby, to the north of Copenhagen, is of especial interest in this connection. On the cobbled floor of the stone cist were scattered burnt bones overlaid by a man's dress. Among the grave goods, which included a sword and a brooch, was found a leather bag containing a series of amulets. The buried man must have enlisted the help of a magician; or he might have been able, himself, to release the powers of the amulets. This is not the only find of its kind from the period and a select list of the objects found in similar bags recalls the witches' brew described in *Macbeth*: vertebrae of snakes, a falcon's talon, a bone from the foot of a lynx, small stones in a bladder, fragments of iron pyrites, part of a bird's gullet, the lower jaw of a squirrel and a series of small sticks bound with cord. Unfortunately we cannot interpret the virtue and value of this strange mixture.

Plate 41

In the third period of the Bronze Age, the first simple examples of the wind-instruments known as *lurer* appear, but we will discuss them in connection with the later, more elaborate, examples which belong to the Late Bronze Age (Periods IV–VI).

During the fourth period of the Bronze Age, cremation is the prevailing burial custom and the burnt bones are most commonly deposited in the ground in burial urns. Stone cists are occasionally found but they are usually of smaller size than those discovered in the previous period.

The burial urns or cists were placed either directly in the ground or secondarily in barrows. In one urn from the Late Bronze Age (we cannot give it a closer date) were found the cremated bones of a young man or woman with the wings of four birds, three pairs from jackdaws and one from a crow or rook. Such a find can give us some insight into the minds of the people who buried this young person; for it is safe to assume from it that they believed that man after death would wing his way into the hereafter. Such ideas are not unknown in modern, civilized society and the simile of birds' wings is used, for instance, in a popular Danish funeral hymn to this day.

The bogs have produced the richest finds of this period. Women deposited large, ribbed neck-rings in them, perhaps as a symbol of thanksgiving, perhaps as a symbol of expectation, perhaps as an offering to a god or a goddess. A remarkable find that can probably be ascribed to this period is a whole flotilla of small boats of gold, ornamented with concentric circles. But the most remarkable and astonishing finds of the period are those of *lurer*, gold bowls and weapons.

The *lurer* appeared for the first time, as we have seen, in the previous period. But then they were simple instruments; now they have developed into impressive, fully-developed instruments with large twisted tubes. Thirty-one *lurer* have been found in Denmark and, although several have been found in

Plate 44

neighbouring countries, it is evident that the instrument is a Danish invention. The casting of such implements was a very complex process carried out by the *cire perdue* (the lost wax) method: the desired part was modelled in wax over a clay core and covered with another layer of clay; pins of bronze kept the two clay parts separate when the wax was melted and allowed to run away through holes in the outer casing. The molten bronze was then poured into the empty space and when the whole thing had cooled down the moulds were broken or cut away from the bronze. The *lurer* were cast in individual pieces and the chain and the dangling plates were made separately. The different parts of the tube were joined together, and care had to be taken that the metal of the rings used for joining was of a lower melting point than that of the metal used in the tubes. In order that the *lur* might be more easily handled the lower portion was detachable and the two pieces could be fitted together and locked by a simple device. An amazingly high degree of technical skill was needed, and an enormous amount of metallurgical knowledge must have been available to the craftsmen who made these *lurer*.

It is noticeable that *lurer* are usually found in pairs of similar size and tone. As musical instruments they are quite impressive, even if the noises they produce can hardly be called beautiful. When they were first found it was thought that only the basic notes of the scale could be played on them, and the playing of songs without the intermediate notes gave the performance a certain quaint, primeval charm; but recent experiments have shown that they can produce a complete register of notes. Modern songs have been played on these ancient instruments and modern composers have even used the tonal range of the *lur* in large orchestral pieces, though without great success. When two *lurer* are played together the resulting music has greater power and resonance: nevertheless, it is unlikely that Bronze Age executants engaged in ensemble playing.

The tone produced by the *lur* is soft and resounding, and may be compared with that produced by the larger modern wind-instruments. The round plate at the mouth of the *lur* is decorated, often with a ring of bosses divided by concentric circles. The small pendant plates, attached to a number of small loops on the mouthpiece, added a shrill tinkling to the sonorous tone of the *lur*.

Another rich yield from the bogs are the gold bowls of which no less than eight large finds have been made. At Lavindsgård, Funen, eleven gold bowls and a large bronze vessel with punched decoration were found. The fact that these bowls were shaped by hammering indicates that they were imported from Western or Central Europe, as the technique is unknown in the North. But the handles of the bowls with their strange horned horses' heads had been added to the bowls in Denmark. This is not the last time that we shall meet the horned horses.

Among the finds of weapons in this period are a number of large circular shields in hammered bronze. All these shields were imported and the crescent-shaped indentation in the bosses of some specimens is perhaps an indication that they came from the South.

The same is true of the horned helmets, executed in a similar manner, found during peat-cutting in the Second World War at Vixø, Central Zealand. These helmets are terrifying adornments for great warriors: in the centre of the cap is a rib with a groove which would hold a crest or panache and on either side is a curved horn; the central rib continues between two large eyes of horrifying size and aspect and terminates in a curved beak, the whole giving the impression of a stylized head of a bird of prey. Rows of small dots outline further birds' heads. Heads such as these are a common ornamental feature on bronzes from Central Europe. Horned helmets occur over a wide area of Bronze Age Europe, reproductions having been found, for instance, in Sardinia. It is interesting that a small Danish bronze figure of a man is adorned with a horned helmet, which demonstrates that such helmets were not uncommon in Denmark. The helmets with the shields, *lurer* and gold bowls, on the other hand, can only have belonged to the upper classes. It was presumably members of the same class that wore the heavy gold armlets—heavy rings terminating in globular or cup-shaped knobs.

More common in the graves of women are the belt-boxes which we have encountered in the earlier periods. These have now grown much larger and have a domed base. The brooches are also larger and the ribbed bow has developed large domed plates at either end, giving the brooch the appearance of a pair of enormous spectacles.

Plate 38

Plate 34

The men's graves often contain long swords, more solid weapons than those we have seen in earlier periods, designed for cutting as well as thrusting and with a T- or kidney-shaped termination where the hilt meets the blade. Some of the urn burials contain miniature swords of this type placed there as symbols of the real ones which would not fit into the urn but which were still necessary to the man in the after-life. There is often a razor in the man's grave, such as the one decorated with one of the favourite motifs of the period: a ship, long and slender, with an elegantly curved ram at the stern. Other toilet articles are tweezers, combs and tattoo needles (or awls). All these must have been rather painful implements; the blunt razors, for instance, must have made shaving rather unpleasant and as there was no soap, grease or oil probably served the purpose instead.

Plate 45

The fifth period of the Bronze Age has been characterized as the Baroque period. The ornamental motifs consisted of strongly curving, wavy ribbons; the belt-boxes had grown so enormous that they must have been extremely uncomfortable personal ornaments and the neck-rings and brooches were also huge.

The ornaments may have been heavy to wear but they must have afforded their wearers considerable satisfaction as no one could fail to be impressed by the rich display.

We have an interesting votive find from this period (*c.* 800–600 B.C.), which came from a well at Bundsene on the island of Møen. The well was lined with the hollow trunk of an alder and with a series of stones, and in it were a number of objects from the Late Bronze Age. It contained a number of hanging bowls (or belt-boxes), a belt-buckle and three bronze spirals as well as the bones of two oxen, three calves, a horse, a pig and a dog. It seems possible that Bronze Age man believed that there was a power in, or behind, running water; a water-nymph, perhaps, who regularly provided clear drinking water.

There are very few finds representative of the end of the Bronze Age, but some votive offerings give us interesting information about the connections between Denmark and the countries which lay to the south. The cremation burials of the period have produced very few objects—a handful of pins and a few other small articles. Two types of urn from this period are of rather unusual shape, one is formed as the model of a house and the other is decorated with a human mask. The urn was evidently considered as a home for the dead. Apart from the urn other types of cremation appear during this period; for example, traces of burnt layers and pits are found on the old ground surface or around urns in which a few of the burnt bones from the cremation are placed.

During this period our knowledge of the ornaments, tools and weapons is derived from votive deposits. Enormous twisted neck- and arm-rings are still to be found and large curved pins are found side by side with smaller elegant swan's-neck pins. The bronze objects of this period provide ample evidence of contact with Europe south of the Baltic, and such objects as the swan's-neck pins and the tanged swords owe their origin to the Central European Iron Age Hallstatt

Plate 43

Plate 37

culture. The bronze swords of the Hallstatt type are copied from bronze or iron prototypes, the design of the swords having reached Denmark before the arrival of the knowledge of iron.

Hallstatt, the place which has given its name to the earliest phases of the Central European Iron Age, is in Austria and achieved economic importance in this period because of the salt which was mined in the vicinity and which formed an important trading commodity. It is situated in a valley high up in the Austrian mountains, accessible only by narrow paths, but the demand for salt in this period was so great that the inaccessibility of the place was no drawback as far as its economy was concerned. The salt that was mined at Hallstatt was carried down the mountains and distributed over a wide area so that Hallstatt became a rich place, inhabited by specialists, who, despite the fact that they had to buy all their food at the foot of the mountains, were able to afford luxuries—bronze vessels from Italy and amber from Scandinavia—luxuries which may have compensated in some small way for the discomforts of their hard life in the mountains and the dampness of the mines.

Hallstatt illustrates the importance of trade in this period, but we have less knowledge of that carried out between Denmark and Central Europe in exchange for the weapons and ornaments that flooded the country. Perhaps Denmark was already obtaining its main income from the export of dairy and farm produce to areas with poorer agricultural land.

But despite our great knowledge of the rich material culture of the period, it is a one-sided knowledge where Bronze Age Denmark is concerned. We have no knowledge of the houses the people built. We have certain Late Bronze Age finds which give us a little information about the settlements of the people but, although such relics as pottery crucibles and soapstone and clay moulds for casting throw a little light on the economic life of the people, it is difficult to conjure up an impression of the daily life of the farmer. This is, however, possible in the following period and there is no reason to believe that living conditions underwent a fundamental change.

So far we have only touched lightly on the works of art of Bronze Age date when we discussed the Trundholm sun-chariot. In the later periods the art develops in two media—bronze and stone.

The miniature cast-bronze statues of this period may seem naïve to modern eyes, but they are original creations of artists. Let us look briefly at two groups of cast figures. Firstly, those from Fårdal in North Jutland, where a group of horned animal heads were found. Two of the heads, facing in opposite direc-tions, are joined together with a small bird perching between them. Also in the group was a small kneeling female figure dressed only in a cord skirt and a neck-ring, with a lifted arm which at one time had obviously grasped something, its eyes emphasized with gold inlay. Another figure from the find is a sinuous snake with a horse's head and a crest. All the figures have lugs at their base, by which they were probably attached to a wooden or metal platform. It is tempting to picture the woman as a goddess, with a snake familiar, to whom offerings of neck-rings and plaited hair were made.

Another strange find was made in the eighteenth century in Grevens Vænge, near Næstved in South Zealand. For many years the find and all knowledge of it was lost, but recently two contemporary drawings were found and two of the six figures were traced amongst the National Museum's collections. The find originally consisted of three female figures, clothed in cord skirts, wearing neck-rings and leaning backwards, and the two figures of men with horned helmets (comparable with the helmets from Vixø) in a kneeling position. The men hold an axe (of a type known in coeval Danish archaeological material) in one hand while the other hand rests on the stomach. The sixth figure is of a woman in a long skirt, with one hand stretched out and the other on her stomach. The whole group looks like an arrested scene from a play. The kneeling men with axes are reminiscent of later Lapp representations of the pre-Christian gods of Scandinavia; but comparisons such as this, spanning such a long period of time, are dangerous and liable to misinterpretation.

The artist who worked in stone at this period was not a sculptor, but a delineator or draughtsman. His work is to be seen on loose stones or boulders and, in Bornholm alone, on the living rock. The carvings are rather monotonous, the commonest motif being a simple hollow, or cup-mark, in the stone, but occasionally spoked wheels, foot-marks and, more rarely, ships are found. The representations of ships are rather simple and consist, usually, of two parallel curved lines connected by short transverse lines; sometimes the crew is represented in a simple and formal manner. Human figures are occasionally carved on the rock, and another motif is a hand with four lines drawn above it.

These rock-engravings cannot have been without significance. The wheel has been interpreted, by Near Eastern parallels, as a symbol of the sun. More important and varied rock-engravings are known from Southern and Central Scandinavia. The drawings here are varied—fights between mounted horsemen, for instance, and many other motifs are to be seen, including large and small human figures standing side by side: sometimes the larger figures have an enormous hand. Carts and ploughing oxen can be seen and even the furrows of the ploughed field are shown. The rock-engravings can be dated, partly by means of the weapons and axes which occur on certain rocks, and partly by the ship types known from the razors (Plate 45), to the Late Bronze Age.

In the ploughing scene the sexual characteristics of the man guiding the plough are accentuated and this, taken with the act of ploughing, must be interpreted as a symbol of fertility.

Fertility, at this period, was obviously regarded as an important power which revealed itself in the raising of crops and the propagation of animals and men. Beliefs concerning fertility can be recognized in a number of finds from the period; on the lid of an urn (dated to the Late Bronze Age by means of the representation of a neck-ring encircling the lid) is a panel which shows a man and a woman, with emphasized sexual characteristics, beside a primitive tree. A slightly later find is a

Plate 47

phallic figure of a man, carved in wood and found in a bog at Broddenbjerg, near Viborg in North Jutland. It was found in a heap of stones associated with simple pottery which dates from the beginning of the Iron Age. A similar figure, though this time female, was found in another North Jutland bog. The special interest taken in the sexual parts of the Broddenbjerg figure is further accentuated by the dark substance (perhaps resin) applied to the abdomen.

We can see behind such figures and representations as these the common attitude of the Late Bronze Age and Early Iron Age people towards the fertility of plants and living creatures as represented, apparently, by their gods.

The ancient sagas of the North associate the gods Njord, Frey and Freja with fertility cults. Now, Njord is related to the god Nerthus mentioned by Tacitus. This reference by the Roman historian of the first century A.D. suggests a definite link between Nerthus and those ungainly but expressive figures of the Late Bronze and Early Iron Ages (cf. page 90).

The Pre-Roman Iron Age

A SCARCITY OF FINDS blurs the transitional stages
between the Bronze Age and the Iron Age in Denmark. The bogs have revealed only a few objects of little
distinction, such as the simple looped ring. Fortunately the
remains of houses on settlement sites and the extensive cemeteries, which occasionally were in use for long stretches of time,
enable us to gather some information about this period.

Conditions cannot have been easy in the early years of the
Iron Age. The new techniques involved in the working of iron
made great demands on the skill of the smith, for the extraction
and working of iron is very different from the equivalent pro-
cesses in bronze-working. The smith who was to work with
the new material needed long training in the details of his
trade—he had to learn the correct moment for the removal of
the metal from the smelting furnace, how and when to use a
hammer and how to weld two pieces of iron together—in short
his craft demanded a tradition and could not be picked up
overnight by rule-of-thumb methods. It is therefore remarkable
that the smiths ceased to manufacture bronze tools and weapons,
although in some ways it is not altogether surprising. Bronze
was only used by the wealthier people during the Bronze Age;
it was an expensive material and had to be imported, the poorer
people used tools of flint, wood and bone. During the Iron
Age not only does bronze disappear as a material of general
utility, but flint also.

The scarcity of bronze may be ascribed to the decline of
trade between Denmark and countries to the south and west.
It is conspicuous that during the early part of the Pre-Roman
Iron Age (400–300 B.C.) the design of the various objects is
based on Late Bronze Age traditions, a feature that is also

evident in the other countries south of the Baltic. The swan's neck pin which we recognized as a Late Bronze Age type develops into the roll-headed pin, often with a flattened head. The belt-hooks are simple catches engaging a hole in the belt and the other ornaments are similarly modest and traditional in design—only the advent of iron tells us that this is a new age.

Many theories have been put forward in an attempt to explain the poverty of the age and the decline in the quality of the finds. One theory that has received considerable support connects this decline with the deterioration of climate that took place at the beginning of the Iron Age, a deterioration due to the pleasant mild climate of the Danish Bronze Age being replaced by wetter and colder conditions. But it is by no means certain that this change, amounting to a drop in the average temperature of a few degrees, was responsible for a cultural decline. It is very much more probable that the Celtic peoples, who at this time dominated Central and Western Europe, were more interested in trade with the Mediterranean area where the aristocracy could purchase such attractive products as wine, beautiful bronzes and painted vases. The trade with Scandinavia was allowed to stagnate—a fact which accounts for the poverty-stricken character of the Early Danish Iron Age.

We have plenty of evidence regarding the burial customs of the Early Iron Age. The body was first cremated and the ashes were placed with the grave goods (which were often simple objects) in a pit; alternatively, the bones were separated from the general ash and placed in an urn which was then buried. Sometimes the urn was placed in the pit which held the ashes (cf. Plate 43). There is also evidence from the island of Bornholm that a barrow has been thrown up on top of the actual site of the pyre, a phenomenon that will be discussed below.

Cemeteries of this period have been investigated in detail in three areas: South Jutland, Funen and Bornholm. The graves, often gathered together in large cemeteries, are either covered by

Plate 40

low mounds, as at Årre and Uldal in Jutland, or form simple flat graves with no barrow. At Årre the earliest graves are in the centre of the cemetery while the later ones spread out around them—a natural distribution when one considers the large area covered by these low, broad mounds. This feature has a chrono-logical significance for the archaeologist, as it allows the dating of certain types of objects by their position in the cemetery in relation to the central, oldest graves.

Further archaeological evidence is provided by the burials at the Mandhøj cemetery on Bornholm, which are placed on top of one another just as were those of the Single-Grave people of the Stone Age described earlier. The first burial in the barrows of this cemetery consisted of a stone circle surrounding the burial or the pyre in the centre; all forms of cremation burial are found and appear to have been used indiscriminately at this early period. On top of this grave was another burial, and later burials were placed above this, and so on. Since with each burial a fresh layer of stones and earth was added, the barrow grew in height with each addition. Only in the cemetery's latest phase were cremation pits placed side by side just under the surface of the area outside the barrows.

Fig. 11 is a sketch showing some of the phases of burial at Mandhøj. In the first phase the pyre is burnt, leaving the char-coal and charred logs, amongst which lie the discoloured and fire-damaged grave goods—potsherds, for instance, burnt red by the fire. A large pyre was not necessary; experiments have shown that a pile of wood about eight or nine feet high, seven feet long and six feet across was all that was needed. In a moderate wind a considerable heat was engendered and the bones split into the characteristic splinters which are found in the cremation graves. *Fig. 11*

Certain of these low barrows have produced the remains of a tent-like structure which had been erected over the grave to form some sort of a mortuary house. The tent was burnt down, *Plates 40 and 42*

Fig. 11

apparently after a comparatively short period and the remains were covered with earth. Plate 42 shows the well-preserved wooden structure as it survived in a collapsed state in one of the barrows. A section through these posts shows that only the outer shell, and not the core of the post, was reduced to charcoal, which points to the fact that the posts were standing and not lying flat when they were burnt. The tent probably collapsed because the roof was made of some highly inflammable material, such as straw. This would quickly burn through the tops of the posts, which would then fall inwards and remain smouldering on the ground. The fire seems to have died out quite quickly in this case—perhaps there was a sudden shower.

We have seen that during the Bronze Age there is some evidence of buildings having been erected over graves; this feature occasionally survives in the later periods. Mandhøj provides clear evidence of the construction and character of the house but its significance is problematic.

From Old Indian sources and from ancient tales in out-of-the-way parts of Northern Europe we learn of a strange state that is said to succeed death, when man becomes a 'wandering soul'; this represented a temporary intermediate stage between life and the final destination of the soul. It was believed that the soul does not reach its ultimate resting-place for some time after death and it is possible that a similar idea was present in the minds of the men who built this temporary house at Mandhøj. It may also have been responsible for the presence of the vessel on the pyre, for the pot seems to have contained food, which was probably needed to sustain the soul on its journey to the after-life. The act of cremation itself was perhaps meant to help the soul on its journey from the body, and if we follow such an analogy to its logical conclusion it is possible that the burnt house followed the soul of the dead man to its ultimate destination. Though we cannot read the thoughts of the people who carried out the cremation and burial, we can, by analogy and

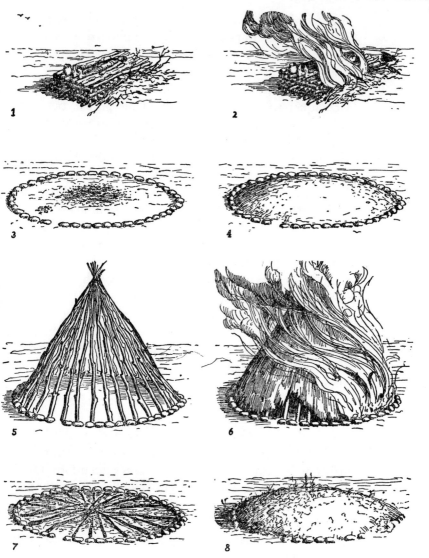

Fig. 11. Reconstruction of a funeral and a mortuary house at Mandhøj.

cautious interpretation of the archaeological evidence, gain some idea of the importance of the complicated ceremony to the people who took such trouble to see that it was properly carried out.

The settlement sites tell us much about the building techniques and general economy of the people, but they are difficult to date with accuracy. However, as no great changes appear to have taken place during the Pre-Roman Iron Age, we shall return to this matter at the end of the chapter.

The middle of the period (about 200 B.C.) has produced an important and interesting find from a small bog at Hjortspring, on the island of Als. This is of special interest in the absence of any important material from the majority of graves of this period.

While working in the narrow strip of peat of the bog, peat-cutters turned up a number of objects: long pieces of wood and weapons and tools mainly of wood, although a few were of iron or bronze. Careful excavation revealed that the bog held a long boat, which was reconstructed with great difficulty from the collapsed remains brought to Copenhagen by the excavator. The most interesting feature was that the stem and stern of the boat terminated in the ram-like feature that we have already noticed in the Bronze Age rock-engravings.

Plate 49

The scarcity of iron in this period is indicated by the absence of this metal in the construction of the boat and of the many shields that were found with it. Nevertheless, the boat was carefully and efficiently built, the different parts being tied together as in skin boats. The five strakes which form the sides and bottom of the boat were cut skilfully with an adze and cleats left at convenient intervals along the planks. These low transverse ridges were pierced by holes, and by means of these the strakes were tied to the ribs. The strakes were tied together with cord and the holes left (by the stitches and seams) after this was done were caulked with resin. This method of boat-building achieved a lightness and elasticity that would enable it to stand up to battering by the waves of the more sheltered parts of the Danish coast. The ribs were reinforced by strong cross-struts, which helped to keep the boat in shape. It was propelled by paddles and steered by a large oar at the stern.

The Hjortspring boat is about fifty-eight feet in over-all length and would carry about twenty men. Assuming each paddler carried a shield and sword, its appearance would be that of a war-canoe. Many weapons were found with the boat—a hundred and fifty shields, a hundred and sixty-nine spears (of which thirty-one had bone heads), but only eight iron swords. A few domestic objects were found with the boat: a spindle, a baking plate and a bronze pin, the latter providing important dating evidence. The wooden shield-bosses are of local manu-facture but they imitate an Early Celtic type made of iron. They are of pointed oval shape and the design of the metal prototype is so slavishly followed that even the rivets (functional where metal is used) are copied in wood on each boss, an effect that is heightened on one example by the addition of two function-less metal nails. These shields indicate that there was a certain amount of contact with the Celts of Central and Western Europe, even if this contact did not result in increased trade.

But this contact is not limited to the imitation of Celtic features on locally manufactured objects, for one magnificent imported Celtic object reached Denmark in the middle of the Pre-Roman Iron Age: the bronze cauldron from Brå, East Jutland. This was found in 1953 in a pit, broken into many fragments. The heavy iron rim was nearly three feet in diameter and the body of the cauldron was decorated with six cast-bronze ox-heads. The vessel was suspended by three large iron rings which were attached to it by heavy cast-bronze owl-heads. The heads of animals and birds on this cauldron are among the very best ornaments produced by Celtic artists.

Plate 48

The gentle ox-heads and the grim owls suggest a strange contrast of temperament. The feather-crests of the owl-heads develop into a stylized, asymmetrical tendril. The animal-heads are paralleled in an object from Brno, Moravia, and we may regard this area as the original home of the cauldron, in which case it must have travelled a considerable distance to reach Denmark.

Boats were not the only method of transport in this period; we have evidence that carts travelled along the primitive roads —little more than cart-tracks—that traversed hill and plain. In some cases, when for instance a road led through a marshy place or when it led to an inhabited hillock in the middle of a bog (as at Borremose, North Jutland), the tracks were carefully cobbled. Such a road, similar to that at Borremose, exists at Tibirke in North Zealand and is closely paralleled by a later road at Broskov which is joined at intervals by a number of sunken by-roads. These two roads have a pavement apart from the road proper. The two roads at Borremose and Tibirke are dated to the middle of the Pre-Roman Iron Age; the one because it leads to a settlement of that period and the other because it has produced objects from that period which had been dropped and trodden into the road.

Plate 52
Plate 53

The theory that these roads were built for use by carts is confirmed by the large number of bog-finds of parts, especially wheels, of such vehicles, which seem in the main to be dated to the Pre-Roman Iron Age. Apart from the simple, heavy wheels, the remains of two substantial and elegant carts have been found which belong to the period just before the Birth of Christ. The carts were certainly made by the most skilful cart-wrights of the period—the Celts. The Celtic craftsmen made many different types of vehicles, some with two, some with four wheels. It is significant that the Romans copied some of their designs, at the same time borrowing the old Celtic names.

The two vehicles were found in a bog at Dejbjerg, West

Jutland. The sides and poles were covered by openwork bronze mountings, a glittering decoration fashionable at the time. Each cart was further decorated with human masks below the curious vertical posts above the side boards. There are numerous domed bosses with triangular and lattice decoration typical of the period.

The wheels are of sturdy design and are bound by iron tyres; the hubs, which have been turned on a lathe, are bound with cast-bronze rings of V-shaped cross-section. Between the hub and the axle is an ingenious device which serves the same purpose as modern ball-bearings; it consists of round, hard pegs that rotate quite easily in the hubs. These help the wheels to turn more smoothly.

The horses were harnessed to a pole, which was attached to the chassis of the cart. As there are two uprights attached to the cross-pieces of the chassis above the hubs, the cart was not very manœuvrable. In order to turn it the side pieces had to be lifted, otherwise the uprights would strike them. There is some evidence that provision was made for such a movement, for various hooks and signs of wear suggest that the side boards were slung on a leather strap.

Carts or wagons like this must have been exceptional vehicles, available only to a favoured few, for only the rich could afford them. Remains of similar vehicles, much damaged from the firing of funeral pyres, have been found in two Danish graves, one at Kraghede (grave A.1), in North Jutland and the other at Langå, South Funen. We shall return later to a discussion of the contents of these graves.

Because of the finds in these bogs and graves we have a greater knowledge of the technique of the Celtic cartwrights from Denmark than we have from the Celtic area itself. This is due, of course, to the religious practices of the Danes, who deposited objects in lakes and bogs, perhaps as a sacrifice to their gods. In this connection it is interesting to recall that

Tacitus—who wrote his *Germania* a hundred years later, basing it in part on older sources—described a religous ceremony in which a cart fulfils an important function. The ceremony took place near a lake on an island to the north of Germany proper, and probably in part of Denmark.

> 'In an island of the Ocean stands a sacred grove, and in the grove stands a car draped with a cloth, which none but the priest may touch. The priest can feel the presence of the goddess in the holy of holies, and attends her, in deepest reverence, as her car is drawn by kine. Then follow days of rejoicing and merry-making in every place that she honours with her advent and stay. No one goes to war; no one takes up arms; every object of iron is locked away; then, and then only, are peace and quiet known and prized, until the goddess is again restored to her temple by the priest, when she has had her fill of the society of men. After that, the car, the cloth, and, believe it if you will, the goddess herself, are washed clean in a secluded lake. This service is performed by slaves, who are immediately afterwards drowned in the lake.'[1]

This strange tale has more in common with ancient Scandinavian culture than have the carts themselves. Tacitus calls the goddess Nerthus and philologists have demonstrated that, owing to a sound change which took place in the period between the time when Tacitus records the name and its first appearance in Scandinavian written records, it is possible to identify Nerthus with the god known to the Norse of later times as Njord. Njord was a god of a fertility cult and we have already mentioned his name in connection with the bog-finds (in a slightly earlier period) of huge wooden figures with emphasized sexual characteristics.

Plate 47

The bogs, however, reveal finds which are more exciting

[1] *On Britain and Germany*, trans. H. Mattingly, Penguin Books, 1948.

still. On several occasions peat-cutters have discovered bodies in the Danish bogs. They can be dated either by the objects found with them or by their position in the bog. Some of the bodies can be dated to the Pre-Roman Iron Age, a dating confirmed by unexpected and rather grisly methods. Investigation of the contents of the intestines have revealed that the last meal of at least one man consists of a half-digested porridge made of grain and seeds which flourished in Denmark during this period.

One of the most exciting finds of recent years is the so-called Tollund man. His clean-shaven face presents to modern eyes fine features, a curved nose and a high, lined forehead. His is a face that would not look out of place in present-day Denmark, a face that it is not easy to forget. He was found lying on his side, as if asleep, dressed only in a cloak and a pointed leather cap. Round his neck was the halter by which he had died.

Plate 46

The Tollund man died by hanging and a woman found in a bog at Borremose seems to have been clubbed to death; both these grim finds bear witness to cruel customs. From a later prehistoric period we read of people who were sacrificed by hanging; in other cases we know of people who were killed as a punishment or as a sacrifice to a good harvest: we even know of kings and other prominent persons who were sacrificed in the interest of the community.

Other contemporary votive offerings consist of vessels containing the bones of domestic animals which were probably placed in the bogs and intended as an offering of food for the gods.

The most precious treasure of Danish antiquity is another bog-find. It is the large silver cauldron from Gundestrup, North Jutland, which was originally deposited on the surface of a small bog. We can scarcely imagine a better example of the respect shown towards the sacred objects which had been offered to the gods. The people of the period were well aware

Plate 55

of the hidden wealth of the bogs and yet would no more dream of touching this than would modern man if they were fenced in by a high-tension cable.

The Gundestrup cauldron is a fascinating object of a quality outstanding for the period and unique in its cultural context. It has a diameter at the rim of twenty-seven inches, and a rounded bottom. On the silver plates which cover the walls are depicted half-length figures of mighty gods and goddesses, some of whom hold human figures suspended in the air, while others hold fabulous beasts. As a contrast to the bearded gods with their frightening expressions there is a gentle-looking goddess tended by women, one of whom is plaiting her long hair. Depicted in the interior of the cauldron are further strange scenes. The well-known Celtic god Cernunnos, with deer-antlers on his head, is seen holding a penannular ring in one hand and a snake with a ram's head in the other. He is sitting with crossed legs and is flanked by a deer and a wolf. There are other figures on the plate but the god, the deer and the wolf are the central, balanced compositions; the eyes of the animals seem to be fixed with awe on the god. Related representations are to be seen on the earliest Gallo-Roman carved reliefs and it is from these sources that we learn that Cernunnos was a fertility god.

Another of the plates with which the interior of the cauldron is decorated represents a god holding in one hand a wheel which a helmeted warrior also clutches; this evidently symbolizes a god of the heavens who was at the same time a god of war. Later, in Gallo-Roman art, the same god with a wheel appears in the guise of Jupiter. A third plate represents a god receiving a human figure as a sacrifice, while a procession of horsemen and foot-soldiers pass by to the sound of trumpets. The trumpets, with mouths shaped like animal-heads, are seen being played by three men on the right of the plate. The fourth plate depicts a goddess surrounded by wild animals. The two elephants that flank her look rather like oxen with elongated

Plate 54

noses, thick legs and small ears, and it is obvious that the artist had never seen an elephant in the flesh, although he may have seen representations of them, for instance, on Etruscan vases.

The fifth wall-plate and the loose one at the bottom represent scenes from a bullfight. The scene on the bottom plate is of special interest. The bull is pawing the ground while the warrior prepares to stab him in the neck; and there are dogs which, save for one that appears to have been knocked down by the bull and is in a crouching position, are shown running.

The Gundestrup cauldron is of vital importance in our study of the art and religion of the Celts and, although itself not a product of Danish workshops, serves to illustrate some of the thoughts that influenced the people of Scandinavia. A few other Celtic cauldrons have been found in Denmark but they are of poorer quality. We also have a number of Danish bronze sculptures which are evidently inspired by the Celtic art of the Pre-Roman period. Danish weapons and ornaments of this period appear to be based on Celtic designs, proving the close links between Denmark and the South and West. Even a few British coins reached Denmark during this period.

One of the implements recovered from the bogs is the simple plough, known as an *ard*, which is still used in certain parts of the world where agricultural practices are rather backward. It is not so long since the *ard* was used in Scandinavia in preparing fields for certain simple crops—potatoes, for instance.

Pollen analysis has enabled archaeologists to assign some of the *ards* found in the bogs to the Pre-Roman Iron Age. The *ard*, found at Hvorslev, Jutland and illustrated in Fig. 12, is an example of the tool in its simplest form. It is a crook *ard* made from a heavy log of wood with a lateral branch, the log being fashioned as a sole and a handle inserted in it. With this implement furrows were turned. Two examples of a more complicated type, consisting of a slender sole to which was attached a handle set at an angle and known as a spade *ard*, were found

Fig. 12

Fig. 13

at Donneruplund and at Døstrup in Jutland. An arrow-shaped share had been fastened to the Donneruplund specimen. There is evidence of yet another type characterized by coulter and mould-board: the coulter is placed in front of the mould-board which turned the soil over from the side of the furrow. The mould-board was reinforced by the insertion of small pebbles which show signs of heavy wear. This plough may have had a wheel, for we know of such features on later examples; but one traditional type of Scandinavian plough is known to have had a mould-board and no wheel.

The *ard* was probably drawn by oxen, whose strength would be needed to force this primitive plough through the heavy turf and top-soil. They were perhaps harnessed with yokes, for several double yokes designed for a pair of oxen have been found in the bogs. The motif of two oxen drawing an *ard* occurs on a number of the Scandinavian rock-engravings of the Bronze Age.

The deposition of these articles in the bogs poses an intriguing problem, for many of the *ards* that are found are either old and battered implements or are made from soft, unsuitable timber. Why should they have deposited an old or substitute plough in a bog? Was the plough perhaps the votive and symbolic offering to a deity who would appease the weather and bring fertility to crops and beasts?

In Scandinavian folk-culture we find many strange practices which reveal a similar belief in powers that promote fertility. These strange inherited beliefs have disappeared in modern times when statistics, science and fertilizers have taken the place of the old customs.

Before we examine the farming methods of this period, it would be as well to turn our attention to the natural conditions obtaining in Denmark during the Pre-Roman Iron Age. Both the sandy soil and the richer loamy soil was cultivated by the farmers. Examination of the pollen in bogs near prehistoric fields in North Jutland has demonstrated that in the Pre-Roman Iron Age the typical countryside was in a state of transition between forest and moor. The forest was open, a kind of heath with scattered trees, and was suitable for the pasturing of cattle, which would eat both the grass and the leaves from the

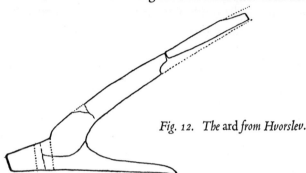

Fig. 12. The ard *from Hvorslev.*

trees. This land was broken by the plough and, when exhausted, was abandoned to the spreading heather. The humid climate of this period gave ideal conditions for the spread of the heather and the beech scrub.

A great number of so-called 'Celtic' fields have been found in Denmark and ascribed to this period. They occur most frequently in Jutland but they are also known on Zealand and Bornholm. The fields are mainly found on the sandy soil which nowadays is abandoned to moor and pine plantations.

There are two methods of dating the fields: by their association with abandoned farms of Early Iron Age date, and by the potsherds found in the banks that surround the field or in the heaps of stones found in it and removed by the ploughman.

The fields are rather small and are square or rectangular in shape. They are surrounded by low banks of earth, sand and stone. A cross-section cut through such a bank often reveals a central core of rich, black earth which frequently yields pottery finds. Excavation of such field banks, which have since been covered by sand, shows that they have not altered greatly since they were first erected. The banks have grown in size through the years, by the addition of stones removed from the centre of the field and by the accumulation of wind-blown earth against this artificial barrier. In some cases a large field has been divided into several small ones and we may perhaps assume that such a division is the result of the division of an inheritance. But there may be a more prosaic reason for the division, for the farmer may simply have wanted to grow more than one crop at the same time. In whatever way we interpret these boundaries, they suggest that the people of the period possessed a strong sense of private property.

Whilst there is, as we have seen, some evidence for the use of the *ard* in the Stone and Bronze Ages, the square or rectangular fields do not appear until the Early Iron Age. They are so similar to those found in the British Isles and other countries of North-west Europe that we may suspect a direct connection between the two areas.

The reasons for the abandonment of the square and rectangular fields are not clear. One theory is that the introduction of the plough with coulter and mould-board made it possible to cultivate the richer, but heavier, clayey soil and that the settlements moved from the poorer to the richer land. It has also been suggested that the abandonment of the fields was due to a major cattle disease.

Some of the abandoned farms were burnt down and, paradoxically, it is from such sites that we obtain the most detailed information about these people's buildings and so about their economy: wood and straw, for instance, will endure in a charred condition, where otherwise they would have rotted away.

Although there are three types of houses in this period they all have a rectangular ground-plan and do not differ fundamentally from one another. The roof is supported by two rows of heavy posts set parallel to the walls. The houses are usually between twelve and eighteen feet broad and the supporting posts stand about three feet away from the walls. These upright posts were probably connected two-and-two by transverse tie-beams which prevented the weight of the roof forcing the posts apart. Their wall structure characterizes the three house types.

Houses of the first type, typified by that from Kraghede,

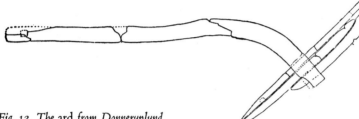

Fig. 13. The ard *from Donneruplund.*

North Jutland, had walls with a framework consisting of heavy uprights, with stakes in between. The heavy uprights helped to support the roof and the walls were finished with wicker-work and the whole structure was then given a liberal coat of daub.

The second type had walls consisting of thin vertical posts finished with wattle and daub. Such walls could not support the roof, which was carried in the main by the rows of heavy posts inside the house; but further support was necessary at the bottom of the roof. During the excavation of a Pre-Roman house at Gørding, West Jutland, a row of shallow post-holes was found outside the walls. The excavator suggests that these holes were made by the rafters which continued down to the ground. Such a method is used today in the traditional Danish *spændhuse*, to which is related the North-west German *varf* where posts are placed at an angle outside the walls and carry a horizontal beam which supports the rafters.

The walls of the third type of house were covered with a pro-tecting layer of turves. Until recently it was thought that the walls were built entirely of turf, but doubt has been cast on this theory by the recent excavation of a *varf* at Tofting in West Schleswig. The walls of this house were built of wattle and daub on vertical posts and only the lower part of the external wall was covered with turf. Traces of such a structure would not be evident unless the houses had been burnt down, but we know of modern houses in Iceland which are built entirely of turf and of houses of Iron Age date from Gotland, Øland and Norway whose walls were probably built of stone and covered by turf. Therefore it is reasonable to assume that the walls of these houses were built either entirely of turf or of wattle and daub and protected at the foot by a low bank of turf.

The ground-plan of such houses is occasionally square, but usually rectangular, in which case it is divided into two rooms. One room, in which the hearth was placed, was the living-room; the other, which was sometimes divided into a series of stalls, was presumably a byre. This plan is seen in the following period, where we have examples of animals being burnt to death in one room of this type of house.

During the last part of the Pre-Roman Iron Age, cremation remains the prevailing burial custom. The commonest form is pit burial, although urn burial also occurs. The grave goods are usually rather poor. In the large cemeteries of the period, which have sometimes produced hundreds of burials, only an occasional belt-hook, triangular brooch or urn is found. A few graves may produce a single potsherd but many only contain cremated bones. A few burials, however, are richer and contain such objects as swords, shield-bosses, crescent-shaped razors or a pair of scissors, all made of iron. The swords are of both single- and two-edged type, the former imitating Celtic types, as do the flat shield-bosses of the period; they demonstrate a continuation of the cultural contacts with the Celts established at an earlier period.

Two graves, because of the exceptional richness of their contents, are especially noteworthy, and it is tempting to imagine that they were graves of chieftains. Both contained four-wheeled carriages with rich bronze mountings which, like the Dejbjerg carts, were of Celtic manufacture. One of these burials (grave A.1 from Kraghede, North Jutland) consisted of a pit containing the bones of two horses and the remains of a chariot. In the cremation pit were found twenty-three pots of excellent quality (one of which is decorated with an ornamental band depicting a hunting scene), three spear-heads, three knives, a buckle and a brooch, all of iron, as well as a plain gold ring. The other grave was found at Langå, Funen, and contained among other things two twisted gold rings, an Etruscan bronze vessel, an iron sword, three daggers, two shield-bosses and two pots. The imported objects in these two graves give us some idea of the far-flung contacts of these presumed chieftains.

It has long been noticed that the pottery from the Kraghede grave and from many other places in North Jutland (the province of Vendsyssel) is closely related to that from the Vistula area and especially to that found in Poznan and Silesia. This relationship has been interpreted by a number of German scholars as indicating an emigration of the Vandals from Vendsyssel in North Jutland to the Continent, where they appear to have occupied the Vistula region during the Roman period. The theory is based mainly upon the similarity between the names Vandal and Vendsyssel; but the evidence is too slender for such far-reaching conclusions. There are in fact in both Vendsyssel (in some of the earlier houses at Kraghede) and on the Continent factors favouring the development of this type of pottery. It seems likely that both areas, which undoubtedly had contact with each other, had a common source for their pottery and general material culture, and that both received their traditions from the Celtic world; although some of the pottery forms may have been derived from the imported Roman bronze vessels. However that may be, cultural contacts and not migrations are mirrored in the finds in the two areas, even though we know of extensive migrations and wanderings in Europe at this period. Just before the beginning of the first century B.C. the Cimbrians and Teutons started their well-known march against Central and Western Europe, and finally even reached Italy. These hardy people, who tobogganed down the Alps on their shields and who fought naked in battle, are said to have originated in Jutland. It is indeed possible that the first small groups set out from Denmark; but if they did, they gathered reinforcements on their way south, as they marched through conquered lands.

Regular trade-routes were now opened up with the South and West and even Roman objects were imported into Denmark. The Roman bronze vessels from this period held wine and were manufactured on a large scale in centres like Capua in southern Italy; they are plain buckets and jugs with an S-shaped profile and a plain handle with a laciniated, or slashed, terminal where it joins the body of the jug. Although several of these Roman vessels were deposited towards the end of the Pre-Roman Iron Age, the Etruscan vessel in the Langå grave is a unique and much older object.

The isolation of Denmark is now ended since she is linked by trade with the Roman Empire. In the period that follows this trade with Rome is so important and dominating that the period is known as the Roman Iron Age.

CHAPTER VI

The Roman Iron Age

IN THE FIRST FEW centuries of our era Denmark had strong ties with the Roman Empire and the new provinces to the west of the Rhine and to the south of the Danube. The natives of these new provinces were mainly Celts; but with the coming of Roman government, craftsmen and merchants moved into the new land alongside the soldiers and the administrators. Industries were founded and quickly flourished, the towns grew in size and importance and the presence of large military establishments offered openings for increased trade.

During the last years of the reign of Augustus the expansionist policy of the Roman Empire, fed on the conquests of Caesar and Augustus, came to an end. The Romans had undoubtedly intended to remove the menace of the Germanic peoples by further conquest but the crushing defeat of the army of Varus at the hands of Arminius and his Teuton followers brought such plans to a halt.

Augustus did not attempt to renew the conflict and by means of treaties with the different Germanic peoples he diplomatically achieved peace. He reasoned that the various tribes would not be able to form large-scale alliances against the Roman Empire as they were too busy indulging in their own private wars and feuds. His assumption was correct, and for two hundred years there was little major trouble between the Romans and the Germanic tribes. It was not until the middle of the third century that the border areas burst into flames and the Romans had to give up their more outlying possessions.

The political and cultural divisions of this era make it convenient to divide the Roman period into two phases, the first lasting until 200 A.D. and the second from 200 to 400 A.D. Let us turn our attention to the first phase.

One of the Germanic tribes with whom the Romans had established contact were the Marcomani of Bohemia, who had only recently moved into the country and conquered it. While the majority of the Celts had moved from the area, a few had remained and, with the influx of traders and craftsmen from the neighbouring provinces, they soon gained cultural predominance in Bohemia. The Celtic craftsmen worked for the Marcomani and the two cultural influences produced certain new types of objects which were to become important during the Roman Iron Age. For example, the brooch with the flat bow, which was developed in this area, spread throughout the Germanic area to Scandinavia. The openwork pattern known as the eyes on the bow of some of these brooches imitates the Celtic *Aucissa* brooch, while on other types an angular openwork pattern on the catch-plate is a Romano-Celtic feature. Other characteristic objects which bear witness to Celtic ability and taste are the buckles and the drinking-horn terminals. The original models of the latter, from which the moulds were taken, were turned on a lathe.

Bohemia became a centre of culture and trade. The rivers Vistula, Oder, Elbe, Weser, Neckar and Lippe formed the basic trade-routes to the North, and of these the Elbe, which reaches the sea to the south of the Jutland peninsula, was the most important to Danish merchants. Communications developed rapidly. The Germanic peoples and the Scandinavians were eager importers of products from the Roman Empire; they had acquired a taste for wine, for instance, and they seem to have used Roman coins. The Romans, for their part, were anxious to obtain products from the North; we know, for example, that one of the commodities in which they were interested was the amber of the Baltic. A Roman knight visiting the Baltic coast in the first century to buy a large quantity of amber, to be used at a great celebration, tells of market-places in which the people gathered to trade and barter.

The large quantities of Roman goods imported into Denmark, including the metal objects which are found in the graves of the period, could only have been acquired in return for a considerable amount of exported goods. The amber and slaves which were traded southwards can hardly have been the sole merchandise involved. It seems likely that the dairy and farm produce (which to this day forms such an important part of the Danish trading economy) was largely exported during the Roman period in the shape of live animals, hides and grain. The problems of transport can have been no more difficult at this time than they were in the Middle Ages, when cattle, poultry and horses were driven southwards along the Jutish roads. A cow would fetch a price high enough to compensate the owner for the difficulties of the journey. Boats loaded with provisions and merchandise would cross the Baltic and sail down the North Sea coast.

This accounts for the majority of the imported objects found in the Danish Roman Iron Age graves; but some of them are rather exceptional and may have reached Denmark for different reasons. A grave found at Hoby, on the island of Lolland, contained two silver cups made by the Greek Cheirisophos that are of the highest quality; they would not have disgraced the table of an emperor or a senator. The quality of the bronzes in the grave is also of a remarkably high standard. The quality of other great treasures in the Germanic area—the Hildesheim treasure, for instance—is inferior to that of the Hoby grave.

Plate 59

Other grave-finds from Denmark contain exceptionally rich objects, such as coloured glass and bronze vessels. These articles cannot be explained simply as the products of trade; it seems likely that they reached Denmark either as the result of robbery or as gifts from Roman statesmen to important chieftains. The name of the owner of the Hoby cups, Silius, is engraved on their bases together with a declaration of weight and the name of the artist (Cheirisophos). We know that an important Roman named C. Silius lived at Mainz at this period and his beautiful set of cups could have found their way to Denmark; we may, however, assume that he did not part with such treasures willingly.

Other objects in the Hoby grave were a flat tray and a series of bronze vessels, a skillet, a plate and a bucket. The scenes depicted on the Hoby cups are taken from Homeric sources. On one cup Priam begs Achilles to yield up his son's body, on the other Odysseus is seen taking the bow of Heracles from the old Philoctetus. The jug is gracefully decorated with a representation of Cupid, drawing his bow, while on the plate Venus is surrounded by Cupids. The skillet bears the manufacturer's stamp, Cn. Trebellius Romanus of Capua.

Many of the Roman vessels found in Denmark come from Capua and their presence is revealing. There are several finds of Roman drinking sets from Denmark—that from Hoby is the best example—providing evidence of a refined society somewhat out of keeping with our traditional view of ancient Germanic manners. We can examine the use of these sets of drinking equipment, consisting of a jug, two cups, a plate and a bucket, in mural paintings and other contemporary sources. The skillet found in the Hoby grave may have been used to warm food or to mull the wine.

It is remarkable that the Germanic graves which contain Roman cups and beakers of either glass or silver also contain drinking-horns. It suggests that the presence in local society of what might be called a 'smart set' did not preclude the use of traditional drinking habits. In fact, it may be asked whether the finer cups were ever used. More likely they were only used on special occasions, and it must have been a very rare occasion indeed when they were filled, after the Roman fashion, with wines of the South. The fact that such objects were deposited in the graves is an indication of the importance that was attached to them. In one of the Juellinge graves on the island of Lolland

Plates 58, 59

was found a rather pathetic example of how highly such im‑
ported objects were prized; a dead woman had been placed in Plate 57
the grave holding in front of her face a Roman strainer, as
though this was one of her most treasured possessions from
which she had not wished to be parted. The ladle belonging
to the strainer had been placed in a bronze bowl, which labora‑
tory tests have shown to have contained a kind of beer. This
woman had been buried with a rich set of grave goods, a gold
ring, silver pins with gold filigree heads, a faceted glass vessel,
two drinking‑horns and a small box with a lock. But a de‑
formed leg showed that, despite her riches, life could not have
been altogether easy for her.

Two horns, deriving from the same animal, found in a bog
in South Jutland, give us additional evidence of the drinking
habits of the period, for one had originally contained mead and
the other beer. These different and stimulating drinks obviously
needed separate vessels and this may explain why the horns,
like the Roman cups, are nearly always found in pairs. Tacitus
rather ruefully describes a Germanic beer or cider‑like drink
as a bastard type of wine, highly distasteful to a Roman palate.
A brew similar to that placed in the Juellinge grave was made
after careful chemical analysis, and we must admit that we
cannot but agree with Tacitus' conclusion.

The terminal mounts of drinking‑horns from a double
burial at Dollerup, in East Jutland, are of special interest.
They are shaped like ox‑heads with elegantly curved horns and
stylized features of a type that was quite popular in con‑ Plate 58
temporary Denmark. The Dollerup grave also contained two
silver cups, probably made in the northern Roman Provinces,
and a series of beautiful bronze vessels which are slightly later
in date than those of the Hoby find, and slightly inferior in
quality. These bronzes demonstrate the gradual degeneration
of Roman taste owing to the growth of the export trade and the
consequent mass‑production necessary to supply the goods.

It is evident that graves like those from Dollerup, Juellinge and Hoby are representative of a rich upper class, as both the imported objects and those locally manufactured give an impression of great wealth. It is to be noticed that the body was not cremated in these rich burials and indeed during this period the practice of inhumation once more becomes popular. The presence of both cremations and inhumations in the same cemetery is an indication that the two practices do not reflect religious or ritual antagonism. But there must be some reason for the quick spread of the practice of inhumation in the years after the Birth of Christ: Roman influence cannot account for this, as cremation was still being practised in Italy. It seems more likely that the rite is due to contact with the Celts; for, although they and other immigrants from the East took over the local cremation practices, we can already see in Central Germany of the Pre-Roman period a number of inhumation burials, presumably carried out under Celtic influence.

Whatever may be the reason for the change, the new rite helps the archaeologist, for the bodies were buried fully clothed, wearing ornaments and jewellery and carrying their weapons. It is interesting to note the position of the ornaments in relation to the body; in countless women's graves a brooch is found on each shoulder, giving some indication of the fashions of dress prevailing at the time. This type of brooch, when found in graves of the first century B.C., conveyed nothing of this, since the bodies had been cremated. We can learn more about how these pairs of brooches were worn from the archaeological record in the Celto-Roman Provinces. In Pannonia, for example, we know that while the men adopted Roman dress the women continued to wear the traditional clothes of the Celts. On the grave-stones of this area we see the man attired like a sophisticated Roman while his wife is clothed in the manner of her ancestors; her costume can perhaps be compared with the modern folk-dresses of European countries. She wore a long gown fastened at each shoulder by a brooch, and it is evident, from the remains found in the graves, that these Celtic gowns were adopted, along with the new brooches, by the Germanic peoples in the first century B.C.

Another feature of the inhumation graves is the set of pottery vessels placed with the dead. The practice of furnishing the graves in this manner is common in East Jutland, where a large number of similarly furnished graves are found, and is not unknown elsewhere in Denmark. Such a typical set of pottery vessels is occasionally encountered in the cremation burials, but their purpose is much more evident in association with an inhumation grave. The vessels are always found in a definite order and it is reasonable to assume that this was the order in which they were placed when a meal was laid. On a large plate placed at the dead person's feet stood a small vessel; by the side of the head was a further series of vessels, a small vase, a handled beaker, a pedestalled beaker (with a small cup inside it) and a larger vessel. It seems likely that there were wooden trays for bread and meat with this service, for the pottery containers would probably only be used to hold liquids. Knives are often found with this array of utensils and we may presuppose the occasional presence of a wooden or horn spoon, of a type that we know only from settlement sites.

Plate 56

Another set, found on Bornholm, demonstrated the high quality of the pottery of this period and the importance that was attached to the potter's craft. Here were found a large vessel, a jug, a handled bowl and an elegantly rounded, fluted cup, all made from fine, dark clay and of the highest technical quality.

Plate 50

We have already discussed the possible beliefs of the people of the Pre-Roman Iron Age with regard to the after-life, and these richly furnished burials suggest a similar tradition. We must suppose that the dead were thought to need food before reaching their final home. The folk-culture of Scandinavia has always placed great emphasis on the ability of the dead person to partake in his funeral feast. In more recent times, in South Sweden, we have examples of food and drink from the funeral feast being placed, with cutlery, in the coffin before burial. It lends support to our interpretations of the Iron Age burial customs when we see traces surviving to this day in traditional sections of the Scandinavian communities.

But food and drink was not the only equipment placed in the grave to provide for man's departure to the after-life; tools and weapons are also found in the graves. The smith, for example, was sent on his journey with the tools of his profession. The weapons usually found in the graves are a sword, either double- or single-edged (the former imitating the Roman types), a spear and a shield, fitted with an iron boss to take the hand. Even the poor man was buried with a spear.

Numerous settlement sites belonging to this period furnish us with information about the life of the living. But we will consider such material—basically the same as in the previous period—at the end of this chapter.

During this period Danish archaeologists once again owe a great debt to the finds that have been made in the bogs. The commonest finds are weapons, reflecting perhaps something of the spirit of unrest abroad at this time in the countries on the fringes of the Roman Empire.

Towards the end of the first century A.D. the Romans had built up a strong line of defence just to the north of the upper courses of the Rhine and Danube. This line comprised a number of fortresses in front of which was a continuous palisade running from the Rhine, near Coblenz, to the Main, near Frankfurt, and so to the Danube near Regensburg. At intervals along this palisade stood a series of watch-towers. This system of fortification was not designed to prevent a frontal attack by the Germanic tribes, but rather to weaken such an attack and to cut off the retreat of any plundering tribes who might attempt to return with loot to their homes.

This line of defence was continually pierced during the third century and had to be completely abandoned in 260, at which time the Romans retreated to the other side of the Danube and held their position there until the Teutons and Huns broke through at the end of the fourth century.

Great bog-finds, especially those from Thorsbjerg, Vimose, Nydam and Illerup, have produced large quantities of Roman material. Objects such as long swords and the ornamental discs attached to the shoulder-strap, with a few finds of a more elaborate armour, helmets and attachments of helmets, indicate a very close contact with the Roman border area. There are two possible explanations for their presence in the bogs of Denmark: they are either loot from border raids or equipment acquired by a Germanic mercenary serving in the Roman army. We know that large numbers of Germanic warriors were employed as auxiliaries by the Romans and stationed in the outposts, the regular soldiers being stationed behind the lines in the legionary fortresses.

Plate 61

The objects found in the bogs are those that such auxiliary troops would possess. If we compare the material found in the Vimose find, for instance, with the equipment found in the border fortresses, we can see that the Scandinavian's equipment was that of a guerilla, not that of a soldier defending a large permanent fort. The Dane was not interested in the typical weapons of large-scale defence, such as the ballista, or the more complicated military equipment; his first interest was in the long sword, the weapon of the cavalryman. These swords were made from hard steel in large factories. They were Celtic in style, a fact that is not surprising when we consider that a large number of Roman smiths and auxiliaries were Celts. The Germanic and Scandinavian tribes adopted this weapon— which was not merely effective, but had become a necessity— in the Late Roman period. In the earlier period the barbarians had had to contend with the Roman legionary with his short slashing sword, but later they met the auxiliary who used the long Celtic weapon. In order to survive, they followed his example. The Germanic tribes also copied the Roman tradition in their use of the scabbard, which was slung from the belt through a vertical loop.

Although the contacts of the Dane with the Roman world were often bellicose, this was not their only sort of contact. Vessels of bronze and glass bear witness to more peaceful associations, and certain objects of art in Danish graves point to a contact with the Romano-Celtic world. Furthermore, the runic alphabet of the North is an independent transcription by the Germanic tribes of the Roman alphabet.

Turning once more to the evidence of the graves, let us examine a number of well-equipped examples from Zealand, which must be the last resting-places of wealthy farmers. The graves contain, besides a rich display of locally manufactured objects, quite a few Roman bronze and glass vessels and a number of silver cups (which always appear in pairs). The latter are chalice-shaped, consisting of semicircular bowls set on a high foot with thin raised walls. Below the rim is a gilt border with an ornament consisting of animals, human figures, masks, rosettes, etc., carried out in low relief. Their decoration recalls that of Romano-Celtic reliefs—one of the strange reliefs from the Thorsbjerg bog, for example, shows running deer with their legs bent inwards in a manner characteristic of the animal decoration of the cups. The same technique characterizes a number of ornamental discs. The craftsmen who made these cups were obviously trained in a Romano-Celtic tradition, and they may well have come from the Northern Provinces of the Roman Empire to Zealand, where they would be given better working conditions than those available in the cramped quarters of the average Roman villa.

The bronze and glass vessels and the enamelled ornamentation of this period demonstrate the successful competition of the

Plate 60

Fig. 14

provinces with the products of Italy. Most of the imported objects found in the Danish graves of this period were mass-produced articles from Gaul or the adjacent areas. As the Celts became romanized they learnt to exploit the Roman talents; but they kept their preference for animal ornamentation: strange, twisted, abstract forms in gaudy colours which were taken over

Fig. 14. Deer-figures from one of the Thorsbjerg plates (left) and a Zealand silver beaker (right). Actual size.

by the Germanic tribes, whose ornamental repertoire was influenced by Celtic models.

Not all the imports and influences came from the West, however. Denmark was also brought into contact with the South-East. The find at Brangstrup, on Funen, represents but one of a number of treasure troves containing gold ornaments such as gold-foil vine-leaves and human figures; it included a disc decorated with filigree ornament. Although some of these objects have direct parallels in Hungary, local influence is seen on one of the leaves; here the traditional veining is replaced by a bird's-head motif that is to be found on locally manufactured gold rings and scabbard mountings. The leaf, therefore, can be seen as a Scandinavian copy of a foreign prototype. The bird's head also appears on Scandinavian copies of the originally undecorated Celto-Roman scabbard mountings. In the following period we shall see how this preference for animal ornamentation developed further.

Further evidence of South-Eastern influence is encountered in the finds from a number of richly endowed graves at Årslev, Funen, containing lion masks of chased gold to which are attached chains and pendants set with red semi-precious stones. The pendant ornaments must have tinkled sweetly at the faintest breath of air or the slightest movement. Heavy brooches, ornamented in the same style with red stones set against a background of gold, provide a striking contrast to the sober fashion of the previous period. The fashion was followed by the wealthy ladies of Rome as well as by their opposite numbers in Scandinavia, and one likes to picture the jealousy of those who could not afford the gaudiness of these resplendent jewels.

This preference for the gaudy and colourful was already present in the Celtic taste but the fashion received its impetus from the East. The new style of decoration with semi-precious stones came to Europe via the Danube and South Russia or by way of the Roman Empire.

Most of the ornaments from the Årslev find and many of those from the Brangstrup hoard originated in the Danubian area, reaching Denmark by way of Central Europe.

In other fields besides that of ornament great developments were taking place. The boats of this period were larger and built clinker-fashion with overlapping planks; tools of more specialized use appear and weaving techniques improve. Although the facts of building, dress and economy can be better studied in this period, they underwent no fundamental change. Let us first turn our attention to the new features of the material culture of this period.

From the finds in a bog on Nydam moor we can see that shipbuilding techniques had developed considerably during this period. Several large boats were found in this bog in the middle of the last century together with numerous weapons and ornaments. One of the boats was well enough preserved to have survived removal and can be seen to this day in the Gottorp Castle Museum at Schleswig. It is about seventy feet long and has a draught of about four feet. Eleven heavy planks were used in its construction, one as a keel and the others as strakes, five-a-side; the gunwale was made of two pieces conjoined. The boat was propelled by oars and the fifteen rowlocks on either side indicate that it had a crew of at least thirty-one. Mast and sails were not used, for sailing-boats were not developed in northern waters until the Early Viking period. The boat was steered by means of a heavy oar suspended from the stern on the starboard side, a feature we have already seen on the Hjortspring boat. But the construction of this vessel shows a considerable advance over that of the earlier one, partly owing to the increased supply of iron. The strong clinker-built sides were fastened together with iron nails and the rather impracticable ram was replaced by a high, rising stem-post. In that the boat was rowed and not paddled, the energy of the crew was conserved. The vessel was tall and comparatively strong and would have stood up to the battering of all but the highest seas. It was, however, not yet strong enough in construction to stand an ocean passage in the manner of the later Viking ships.

Plate 72

Plate 49

The axe was still the carpenter's commonest tool and was used effectively in jobs that would demand two or three tools today. Although the plane appeared in this period it was probably reserved for finer work—smoothing the round shafts of spears and arrows, for example. The bogs have yielded such wooden weapons, and bows made of a single piece of wood as well as quivers to hold the arrows.

Clothes, too, have been found in the bogs. The men's dress consisted of a jacket with long sleeves and trousers, the latter also having attachments which acted as stockings. The women's attire consisted of long gowns made of cloth woven in various designs, but only portions of these have been found in the bogs. The clothes found at Thorsbjerg, in particular, illustrate the high quality of weaving in this period—a weaving that developed elegant patterns.

The excavation of a number of settlement sites has given us a great deal of information about the farm and its economy in this period. The most common find consists of the foundations of the house, and occasionally the archaeologist has been lucky enough to find a number of superimposed houses. Jutland, Funen and Bornholm have produced most evidence regarding the houses of this period, although a number of examples are known from Zealand. The building practices are based mainly on those of the Pre-Roman Iron Age; only on Funen do we find a different type of house—a type, incidentally, which was used until quite recently in that area. The Funen house is rectangular in plan with a central row of posts which carried the main roof-beam. The normal house of the period had a roof supported on a double row of posts joined together and strengthened by tie-beams. The excavations at Dalshøj, Bornholm, Fjand, West Jutland and Ginderup, North Jutland, have yielded especially important information about house structure in this period. At Ginderup, for example, one of the houses had evidently been burnt down and the charred remains of the roof lay on the ground. The roof covering was supported on rafters between one and a half and three inches thick. A layer of straw was tied to these rafters and two layers of heather-growing turf were placed over the straw, back to back with the heather surface outwards. Although this house had a turf roof it is possible that others had a lighter, thatched roof.

Another house at Ginderup had to be abandoned in such haste that a number of animals were trapped in the fire and must have been burnt to death. The house was some thirty-eight feet long and fourteen feet wide, the walls having a protective covering of turf, which may have reached up to the roof, while the interior was panelled with wood (cf. the house type mentioned on p. 98 in connection with the Roman Iron Age house at Tofting). The western end of the house had a clay floor and near the square, ornamented hearth were found a quern-stone, a charred wooden spoon and clay vessels containing burnt grain. At the eastern end of the house were traces of a series of partitions, or stalls, and bones bear witness to the fact that this was where the animals were quartered. The remains of four sheep, a pig and a cow were found in this area, and presumably other animals were rescued before the fire became too fierce.

Fjand was an important settlement site and will be discussed further as we proceed. The walls of one of the houses on this site were built of a series of vertical wooden poles whereas all the other houses had wattle and daub walls. Especially interesting was the find on this site of a charred wooden door made of two planks of oak, each about a foot wide, joined together by means of two opposed curves of wood slotted into the boards. The door, which was hung on pivots, is only about four feet high and this gives us some indication of the height of the walls.

House C on the Dalshøj settlement site was found to contain an unusually large number of objects. This house was built in a fertile area, very different from the poor sandy lands of Jutland, and provides us with important evidence concerning the farming economy of the period. While the Jutland sites have yielded only a small amount of grain, here large quantities of burnt barley and oats, of magnificent quality, bear witness to the fertility of the soil around the Dalshøj settlement.

The rectangular plan of the house could be traced by means of the red burnt clay of the walls; at the eastern end was a small room with a gravel floor, which evidently housed the animals, while at the west end a high clay hearth was found with a stone circle to contain the fire. Pottery vessels were standing in and around the hearth. On the floor were iron knives, spindle whorls, loom-weights and brooches which probably came from the dresses which hung on pegs round the walls. Traces of a semicircular baking oven were also found and, although this oven was disused during the last years of the house's occupation, it provides some evidence of the practice of baking bread.

Post-holes revealed that the roof was carried on a double row of posts which were placed in pairs and correspond with the more slender uprights of the walls. The main wall-posts were tied together along the top of the wall by horizontal struts and were also tied to the internal rows of posts, which in turn were tied to one another. In between were secondary vertical posts which were bound together with wattle and daub, some of which was baked hard when the house was burnt down, its complicated pattern of wicker-work revealing the structure of the walls.

The roof was probably pitched at the gable-end, for the interior posts, carrying the main weight of the roof, stop a little way from the end wall. Had the gable wall risen straight up to the roof-beam, we would expect to find heavy posts incor-porated in the structure of the wall, and such a feature is not present here despite the fact that the wall is well built.

The burnt grain and the large number of animal bones found on this site support the view that this was a wealthy farm. Situated as it was in the centre of its fertile fields, a gentle slope provided natural drainage for the fields, the water flowing down the slope and not gathering in marshy patches.

The commonest domestic animal was the cow, and cattle were probably used for draught as well as dairy purposes. What with the meat, skin and horn which they provided at the time of slaughter, they could be considered a very profitable invest-ment. The sheep, which provided wool and meat, was also very common; as was the pig, which was kept in the forest and was somewhat smaller than the normal modern breeds. A couple of goats would probably be kept for dairy purposes and an occasional horse for riding.

Analysis of the burnt grain from the site shows that it was

particularly free from weeds, and the presence of the different grains in separate piles indicates that the different varieties were grown separately. Most of the fields yielded barley, but emmer (a primitive form of wheat) was also cultivated. The ears of corn were cut off high up the straw, which perhaps accounts for the lack of weed in the samples excavated. But the few traces of weeds give us some indication of the condition of the land. Hans Helbæk, who has examined the grain and other seeds, tells us that the fields must have been unevenly drained, with some parts evidently rather wet, while others were drier. The corn therefore grew in irregular patches, but it was healthy and the harvest would be sufficient to last the winter.

But the farmer's life on the sandy fields of Jutland presents a different picture. Here the corn was of poor quality and in order to eke out supplies it was necessary to mix wild seeds with the cultivated grain. On settlement sites near lakes or near the coast, fishing formed an important addition to the economy of the farmer. This overlap of farming and fishing is illustrated by the net-sinkers found on the farming site at Fjand.

We have many traces of fields of this period in Jutland, and those connected with the Fjand houses are of special interest as the field boundaries have been covered by wind-blown sand and the banks, enclosing the fields, seem to have preserved much of their original character. The banks, which were quite low, delimited small fields which covered between a quarter and three-quarters of an acre. On hillsides and slopes the erosion of the top-soil and the buttress-like quality of the banks give a characteristic terraced appearance to the countryside.

At Fjand traces of the work of the *ard* can be seen as dark stripes running criss-cross over the surface of the fields parallel with their boundaries.

The quality of the soil is, however, not the only feature that distinguishes the settlements of Jutland from those of Born-holm. The whole character of certain settlements in Jutland is seen to be different, for there several farms have been found gathered together into a village-like community. This is to be seen at Østerbølle in North Jutland, where the houses form two parallel rows and are surrounded by fields. But although the farm-houses were placed close together, the division of the fields seems to indicate that they were not owned collectively but were private property. There was presumably a feeling of mutual security in such a community where the neighbours could help one another in times of trouble.

On Bornholm, on the other hand, the farms are not found together in such a manner; indeed, this is a feature of the island to this day, for there are no villages. In the eastern parts of the island the pattern of the ancient settlement sites is similar to that of modern farms. There would have been little room for anything but fields and woods between each farm (the primeval forest had long since disappeared). The reason for this scattered settlement can hardly have been the poor quality of the soil, for the land is unusually fertile; rather, it may have been a desire for privacy and seclusion.

Agriculture developed rapidly in the Iron Age; large parts of the country came under the plough and simple roads, little more than cart-tracks, led down from the village towards the sea whence the long ships, filled with merchandise, were rowed down towards the mouths of the great rivers, which were the gateways to Continental Europe.

CHAPTER VII

The Dark Age

THROUGH THE LONG and troublesome years of the fourth century A.D. the Romans had managed to preserve most of their frontiers intact, but in 375 the Roman Empire was invaded by a new and more dangerous enemy—the Huns— and gradually the defence of the frontier changed its character. Germanic tribes invaded the Empire and mingled with the Roman population, until in 476 they gained nominal control of the Western Empire. The Eastern Empire, centred in Constantinople, remained intact, on the other hand, for several centuries.

Among the many tribes that were wandering in Central Europe and South Russia at this period were the Heruli, a tribe which may have originated in Scandinavia. The Heruli are said to have been forced to leave their homes by the Danes and, although we cannot prove this from the archaeological evidence, it is evident that the Scandinavians were interested in the happenings on the Continent. It is likely, therefore, that the Northern people took some part in the proceedings which led to the dissolution of the great Roman Empire. Evidence of contact is provided by the large number of gold coins of Imperial Rome found in the North (especially in the eastern parts of Scandinavia) and by the Scandinavian objects and ornaments found as far afield as Hungary; this points to an intimate relationship between Central Europe and the North. The Roman medals were imitated by the Scandinavians.

Plate 65, centre

The Huns were not the first Eastern tribe to invade Europe and settle in the West, but their arrival was important as it accelerated the inevitable victory of the Germanic tribes over the Romans—a victory that was political and not cultural. The Huns settled in the West and the influence of their distinctive culture can be traced in the finds. Despite the fact that they were an Asiatic nomadic tribe, unaccustomed to European life, they soon adapted themselves to their new surroundings, as can be plainly seen in their negotiations with the Romans. Two conditions appear repeatedly in these negotiations: the Huns would exchange peace for gold and they demanded the right to attend the Roman markets. The Romans would pay them enormous sums of money to leave a country which they threatened to plunder, but some of the gold would be returned to the Romans through the markets, for the Huns were not self-supporting in the matter of food and spices. It was through trade such as this that some of the gold coins of the Empire reached Scandinavia.

Detailed information about the Huns is contained in the description written by an envoy of the East Roman Empire, who gives a lively description of the tribe and its way of life at a period when it was beginning to settle down in Hungary; but this is not the place to discuss these strange, hardy people.

Ultimately it was the Germanic tribes that benefited from the attacks against Rome, for the Huns were finally defeated and their numbers drastically reduced. In the West, kingdoms sprang up in the land once ruled by the Romans and of these the strongest, for many years, was the Merovingian kingdom of France. Roman culture continued undisturbed through all these upheavals and it was only with the coronation of Charlemagne that a new epoch was inaugurated.

At this time raids on the West by the Danes increased in size and importance. During the reign of Hygelac (mentioned by Gregory of Tours) an attack was made on the Frisian coast, but the most important series of raids were those that took place from the North Sea coasts of South Jutland and north-western Germany on the shores of England. Although the British coastal defences were reorganized after the first few attacks, such preparations proved to be inadequate and the invaders flooded into the country. Many of the fifth-century English cemeteries illustrate the close cultural and racial affinities between the North Sea coast and England. The earliest brooches and other ornaments closely resemble those found in the northern European and Rhenish area, and, although the types later develop independently, there is plenty of evidence of contact across the North Sea and of the exchange of ideas as well as goods.

The years between A.D. 400 and 800 are important in European history, but our historical knowledge bears little direct relationship to Denmark. We still depend mainly upon the archaeological records for our understanding of this period of Danish history. Excavations of recent years have revealed that this was a not unexciting period of Danish prehistory; a period in which not only important cultural changes took place but one also of political upheaval and dramatic events, which leave their traces in burnt farms, buried treasure and in the possible evidence of the use of hill-forts.

Both the graves and settlement sites bear witness to a distinct and logical social structure. The community was divided into classes with slaves at the bottom of the ladder and chieftains, even kings, at the top. We have no extremely rich graves in Denmark at this period, but the Sutton Hoo burial found in England and the fine Swedish burials at Vendel and Valsgärde tell of the riches of the chieftains and kings in the related areas. The Danish graves point mainly to a population of wealthy farmers and a poorer substratum. Occasionally, as at Lousgård, Bornholm, a poor burial with trashy grave goods is found on top of a rich grave; such cases suggest that a slave may have been sacrificed to follow his master or mistress into the after-life, where he could serve them as he did on earth. We have evidence of this custom in the Viking period both from the archaeological and historical sources.

Although we know of no grave belonging to a member of the Danish ruling class, we know that great riches in precious

Plate 69

stones and gold were collected. This fact is best illustrated by the golden horns from Gallehus which, with their romantic history, constitute one of the most popular Danish antiquarian finds. They belong to the period of transition between the Roman Iron Age and the Migration period. The two large, heavy horns are made of solid gold and must have been enormously valuable. They are decorated with strange patterns in relief and engraving: human figures, animals, fabulous beasts and curious objects, all set in bands round the two horns. On one of these is an inscription, 'I Lægæst from Holt [?], made the horn'—Lægæst had good reason to be proud of his work.

The two horns, which were found separately in 1639 and 1734 in the same place at Tønder, South Jutland, were stolen a hundred and fifty years ago from the Royal Collection and melted down. This was fortunately not an irreparable loss for drawings survived and we have today a fair idea of the size, shape and decoration of the horns. This decoration represents one of the earliest known examples of Germanic animal ornament, which occurs in this period mainly on brooches and mounts.

Although we know the meaning of some of the motifs on the horns, we cannot understand them as a whole. Many have tried to interpret the many extraordinary figures depicted; for example, the three-headed figure who holds in one hand a ram on a lead and in the other an axe or a hammer, has been taken to be a god. The three-headed god is well known in the Roman-Celtic hierarchy, and in a later Scandinavian tapestry such a god is seen as one of a number of pagan powers attacking Christianity. He was still known, therefore, in the Viking period and may perhaps be identified with Thor. The horns also show a woman holding a drinking-horn, two men playing on a gaming-board, a horseman and a centaur.

The origin and character of the Germanic animal ornament

on these horns is not without interest. The motifs clearly have their origin in the simple, stiff, animal figures of the Roman period, but there is a new spirit present, an obsessional interest in animals. The stylized heads, interlaced bodies, biting jaws and beaks produce a strange and foreign pictorial art, often completely devoid of naturalism. The animal ornament is frequently combined with geometrical chip-carved patterns, the deep relief of which gives the surface a dazzling glitter of light and shade. These chip-carved patterns are directly derived from the Roman art of the Northern Provinces, but it seems that the wholehearted interest in animal ornament may have been inspired from areas in Asia inhabited by nomadic peoples. We know very little about the art of the Huns and the other Asiatic tribes who settled in Europe, but there is a remarkable similarity between the motifs seen in Danish art of the Migration period and those found on the Sarmatian metal work of southern Russia and Siberia. A brooch from Galsted in South Jutland is ornamented with a fabulous beast—a winged lion with a twisted body, the front legs turning in one direction and the back legs in the other—which is closely paralleled in the East.

Plate 70, bottom left

The art of Denmark flourished under the influence of this Eastern art and the art of the Roman Provinces, soon developing into an individual style that is known as the Migration period style. This style, which consists mainly of animal ornament, is characterized by a complete stylization of the motifs, the animals being twisted and deformed so that they completely fill the narrow spaces of the fields that offer themselves for decoration. The style is most clearly seen on the large 'relief brooches' of silver-gilt. The dazzling effect of these brooches was achieved not only by the use of chip-carved ornament but also by means of the contrasting colour of the metal employed and by the addition of inlaid black niello—most commonly in zigzag bands. It is typical of the artist of

Plate 70, bottom left

Plate 70

the Migration period that he should decorate both the edges
and the surface of the brooches with animal motifs. In its
earliest form the only animals on the brooch are those that
appear round the edges, the surface being decorated with
geometrical patterns. A rather later, but strange, brooch is that
from Bornholm which was imported from the Swedish island
of Gotland. Depicted on this brooch is a series of birds' heads,
of grim aspect, each beak digging into the neck of the bird in
front. Fully developed examples of this style are known from
Gummersmark, Zealand, for instance, where it is noteworthy
that there is still some organic connection between the body,
head and limbs of the animal. This feature was soon to be lost,
the animal motif becoming more diffuse.

Fig. 15

Once this phase of ornamentation was passed the animals
were treated in quite a different manner. The style, which
developed about A.D. 600 but had occasionally appeared before
this date, quickly spread throughout Europe, where it is known
as far afield as Ireland, Italy and Sweden. It is formed by the
coalescence of the broken animal ornament into a series of
ribbon-like bands, which are characterized as animals by the
addition of heads, tails and limbs to the long, winding in-
organic bodies. The ornament is abstract in style though based
on the old animal ornament, for it would seem that a liking for
animals lingered on among the artists.

In the seventh century this style was succeeded by two completely different ones; the first was characterized by a triangular
animal motif—a horse or deer with interlaced ribbons—the
second is more complicated and consists basically of animals
forced into the field available for decoration and encompassed
by ribbons and loops of interlace pattern. The animal heads
are of a weird shape and rather stunted, while the bodies sprout
legs and wings, the whole resulting in an elegant and sophisticated linear pattern. This style is seen on the earliest domed oval

Plate 73

brooches that were worn in pairs by the women, one on either shoulder, but it is also found on other objects, as, for example, the unique horseshoe-shaped mount from a grave at Lousgård, Bornholm, where two birds are depicted holding snakes in their claws. This strange mount is gilt and inlaid with garnets and would show up strikingly against the fabric of the dress.

Plate 73

The development of styles provides a rough dating method; another method is based on the study of imported gold coins,

Fig. 15. Mounting decorated with two ribbon-like animals in Style II. Actual size.

Plate 70

which are sometimes found in association with other objects and thus provide the archaeologist with a rough date. We will return to a discussion of this dating method at a later stage. As in the earlier periods, our knowledge of the economic life of the community is derived from the excavated settlement sites. Two houses were found close together at Oxbøl in South-west Jutland, but although we know that they belong to the same period, we cannot be certain that they were intimately connected with each other. The one was long, larger than the houses of the

Roman period, and was divided into three rooms; the other was smaller. The larger house demonstrates that the population of the period felt a need for more room than had been available previously, perhaps because more animals were kept.

A similar impression is gained from farms which have been excavated in the fertile areas of the island of Bornholm. Strangely enough, it seems as though these settlements were abandoned shortly after A.D. 500. Two of the farms investigated consisted of two houses each, one larger than the other. One of the houses was L-shaped and they were all constructed in a fashion similar to that which we have examined in the Roman Iron Age, with low walls of posts, branches and wattle and daub. The roofs were carried on two rows of posts, except in the shorter wing of the L-shaped house where the roof was carried on one row of posts.

Farms were situated on a gentle slope, often near a lake, which would provide both water and peat, as well as some fish. Near the farms were woods in which the pigs could root about for acorns. Oak was a common tree and was often used for building purposes.

There are many finds from these farm sites. The hearth, which was usually raised on a foundation of clay, was placed at one end of the house—in the L-shaped house it was at the angle between the two wings—and most of the finds occur in this area. Iron knives, spindle whorls, pins, brooches, needles, bronze tweezers and long narrow bone combs decorated with punched and incised ornaments, are all plentiful. The remains of a loom were found in one case along one of the short walls, Plate 62 the pottery loom-weights lying undisturbed in a long row leaning against one another. Only a few were found out of place, the others having fallen only a few inches to the floor when the house was burnt down. The loom-weights are of a well-known form: flat with a central hole and an oval cross-section. The loom was of the traditional type described above.

Carbonized grain was found in little piles on the floor, not in such great quantities as in the previous period nor of such purity, as it was mixed with seeds of wild plants. This is rather odd when we consider that the soil on this site is very fertile and would yield a considerable crop; it suggests that there must have been a shortage of grain at this particular time, though this is not accounted for by a bad harvest, for the grain is plump and in good condition. The crop was grown in the surrounding fields where the soil was prepared with a plough that probably had a coulter and a mould-board. The grain was harvested with sickles, possibly scythes, and was ground in a rotary quern, which had succeeded the saddle quern used in the Roman period. This rotary quern, which was used in Central and Western Europe in the pre-Roman era, did not appear in Denmark until much later; it was worked by hand, for there is no hole in the upper stone to take a pole. A burnt-clay oven tells of the use to which some of the grain was put. It was dome-shaped, with a small opening in one side—and perhaps at the top—which was closed when the oven was in use.

The farm animals were still horse, cattle, sheep, goat, pig and dog, with the cattle predominating. On one farm a fox had been kept in captivity, probably as a pet; it had presumably been caught as a cub and its domestication is demonstrated by its teeth, which were worn like those of a dog. All the bones found on this site bore traces of gnawing by dogs and the small marks at the end of each bone indicate that the dogs of this period treated their bones in the same way as do modern dogs.

Charcoal, bones and fire-damaged stones found in pits outside the house tell how these people cooked. The methods were evidently those that are used in primitive societies to this day, the meat being wrapped in green leaves and placed in the pit which was packed with hot stones from the hearth and then covered. After a while the meat could be taken out and the tender joint was ready for eating.

A few bones of a horse were uncovered in a large pit. They differed from the other bones found on the site in that they had not been gnawed by dogs, nor split for marrow and brain. Those found were the skull and foot-bones and it is evident that some special ceremony lies behind their burial. The bog at Rislev, South Zealand, yielded similar finds, dating from the same time; while others from graves in Central Germany and South Russia date from the fourth century and later. Such graves are also found in southern Siberia, where, until quite recently, it was a common custom to raise the hide, head and feet of a horse on a pole as a sacrifice to the supreme god of heaven. Such a practice might well explain the Danish finds, for the bones hanging in the hide on the pole would later be buried as sacred objects. Travellers of the Viking period write of a similar custom in South Russia at that period; here, too, the skin, feet and head of a horse were placed on a pole over the grave of a dead man. It is tempting to interpret this custom, when found in a European context, as resulting from contact with the nomadic tribes, among whom it was a well-established tradition both as part of the burial ritual and as a sacrifice to the gods. The dead man (or the god) was given the soul of the horse, its hide, the beautiful head and the strong feet to serve him in the world of the dead.

Other interesting things were found outside these farms. Near the farm at Dalshøj, for instance, just below the surface of the ground, were found four hoards containing seventeen gold coins, a silver-gilt brooch, three gold rings and a small pierced disc of gold. Outside another farm in the area, at Sorte Muld, a number of coins and some small human figures of gold were found and at places in the vicinity similar finds have been made. Rich hoards of Late Roman coins have been found on other sites.

Plate 70

The human figures, worked in gold foil, represent both men and women, often fully dressed. The men wear trousers and a

Plate 68

jacket or short gown, the women wear a full-length gown and a shawl which falls some distance down the back; occasionally both the gown and the shawl are shown with a braided border of zigzag pattern. One of the little pieces of foil represents two people and is obviously a love scene. Some of the figures are seen to carry staffs with a broad terminal, and we know from Viking literary sources that the staffs were used by a kind of shaman of either sex. This exotic element in Scandinavian religion seems to have come from the East, at what period we cannot tell. Because it is known to have been a prominent feature of Finnish tradition, one theory is that it was introduced during the Viking period as a result of a Finnish influence; but it is equally possible that the shamans appeared at an earlier date, during the Migration period.

The reason for the deposition of so many costly objects in hoards is not immediately obvious—and we must take certain other features into account when we consider the problem. The farms, to which the gold belonged, were burnt down and one of them yielded evidence of a shortage of grain (the cultivated crop being mixed with wild seeds). Spear-heads, not associated with graves, have also been found in the neighbourhood of the farm and a hill-fort was investigated, a short distance away on an uninhabited plot of high ground. The fort consists of a steep-sided rock, the top encircled by a bank with a curved pathway to the entrance. Inside the fort was a natural pool, which would provide drinking-water; pottery found here dates from the Late Roman or Migration periods.

Plate 63

A hill-fort of this type could not have been defended for any protracted period against determined attackers, as the bank is very long and low, but it would give shelter for men and cattle during an invasion or raid. Piles of round, smooth stones were placed inside the bank; these could be thrown and slung at the invaders and they show that the people who took refuge in the camp were ready to defend themselves.

These phenomena taken together can best be explained as a result of a war which took place, according to the coin evidence, during the reign of Anastasius in the early part of the sixth century. The burnt and abandoned farms, the hoards, never reclaimed, and the hill-forts all point to this conclusion.

Plate 64

Many graves of this period produce evidence of considerable wealth; a particularly good example is the recently-excavated grave field at Kyndby in north-western Zealand. The men were buried with weapons of high quality and were sometimes accompanied by their dogs and excellent food—tender joints of lamb, pork and beef. Grave II at Kyndby contained a bent two-edged sword with a gilt hilt, which was decorated with deeply engraved interlaced ribbons and animals. All the weapons from the grave are badly damaged—the shield-bosses are slashed and the sword bent so that none of them could be reused.

Another long-sword, from Bildsø, West Zealand, is also of outstanding quality and is decorated on the pommel with two symmetrical animals.

There are various other personal ornaments apart from the 'relief brooches'—festoons of beads secured at either end by bronze plaques, oval brooches with interlaced animal ornament and elegant brooches in the shape of birds and beaks. The wealthy had more elaborate ornaments, made of gold and in-

Plate 65
Plate 67

laid with garnets. Heavy neck-rings of gold have punched orna-mentation or small gold animals soldered on. These ornaments were designed for the very rich and for the gods. The wooden

Plate 66

statuette wearing three gold rings could be taken as representing a god.

In this period the social structure of Denmark stands out with great clarity. We have evidence of the living conditions of the middle-class farmers and occasionally of the wealthier aristocracy, but we also obtain some impression of the crafts-man's skill—of the art of the smith, the builder and the shipwright. Of these, some were undoubtedly specialists; the swordsmith, for instance, who must have served a long apprenticeship.

As we close this story of Danish prehistory we are approaching the Viking Age and the earliest period of Scandinavia's written history. Missionaries from the Anglo-Saxon area and from Southern Europe bring a new culture and religion to the North. Traces of this appear in the Migration period; in its art we meet an occasional symbol of Christianity, the interlaced ribbon-like ornament, for instance, is ultimately derived from the Near East—from Syria, Palestine and Coptic Egypt. The graves produce bronze mounts which may have come from house-shaped caskets, similar to those brought from the British Isles by the Anglo-Saxon missionaries. With these new ornaments and new objects came new ideas and we begin to find traces of the new religion which in the Viking Age routed the pagan gods, Thor and Odin.

CHAPTER VIII

The Prehistoric Landscape

A S WE LOOK ROUND the Danish countryside we can begin to appreciate the dependence of the prehistoric peoples on their surroundings. The broken coastlines, the straits, the sheltered waters all helped to shape the minds of our early ancestors. The Danish islands are set closely together. From the shores of Als a fire on the island of Funen could be seen quite clearly across the water, and from the Zealand coast the islands of Funen, Langeland and Lolland are visible. Only a narrow strip of water separates Zealand from Falster and Møen, whilst Funen and Jutland are divided by a stretch of water no wider than a broad river. These narrow straits and sounds would have tempted the adventurous, with a result that the waters soon become a link rather than a barrier between different areas; for it was easier for prehistoric man to travel by water than to force his way through trackless forests. This connection is often reflected in the archaeological record; as, for instance, when we find the same cultural traits on sites on either side of a sound, each with a different cultural hinterland.

The first boats were probably made of skins but, as the primeval forest spread over the face of the country, the wooden dug-out canoe was developed. Later on, the two techniques were combined and the wooden planks were sewn together, without the use of a single nail—as in the case of the Hjort-spring boat. Boats of this sort were paddled, and it is not until the Iron Age that rowing-boats, such as the Nydam boat, were introduced. In the Viking Age the introduction of the sea-going sailing-boat resulted in exploration and raiding such as we have come to associate with the Vikings.

The hills and plains of Denmark provided the farmer with widely differing soils. Recent topographical studies have shown

Plates 45
and 49

Plate 72

132

that man's choice between a light and a heavy soil varied from period to period. These topographical studies have been based on a thorough and careful survey of a few selected areas. The areas chosen have been surveyed field by field, every mound has been examined and recorded, every river bank investigated, not a farm has been missed; and the work, though tedious, has produced satisfying results. We find that, during the Neolithic period and the Bronze Age, settlement tended to concentrate on the light sandy soil, while in the Iron Age the farmers turned to heavier, richer soils (although they did not completely abandon the sandy soil). This change can almost certainly be taken as being due to the introduction of new agricultural implements, chiefly the plough with a mouldboard, for the *ard* could only be used with any measure of success on the light sandy soils.

The hunting tribes of the earlier periods lived on low sandbanks near rivers and streams, along the coast or by the lakes. Sometimes their settlements are found on shifting islands in the lakes or on gravel terraces. But in every case they are seen to overlook a wide area of the surrounding countryside.

Other reasons prompted later peoples to build their great burial mounds in a prominent position on the top of a hill or on an eminence by the sea. These barrows, in honour of the dead, were meant to be seen from afar, and were often built along the line of ancient roads. Such features indicate that the living wished to remember the dead and keep some sort of contact with them. There was also perhaps a desire to remind the dead of their old country, the sea and their people.

Plate 29

Farms, burnt or abandoned, tell their story of buildings adapted to the landscape and to the climate. The houses were sheltered from the prevailing winds; in Jutland, for instance, the wild west wind is avoided, while on Bornholm it is the cold east wind that had to be shut out at all costs. In the Iron Age, and perhaps in other periods, too, cattle were provided with

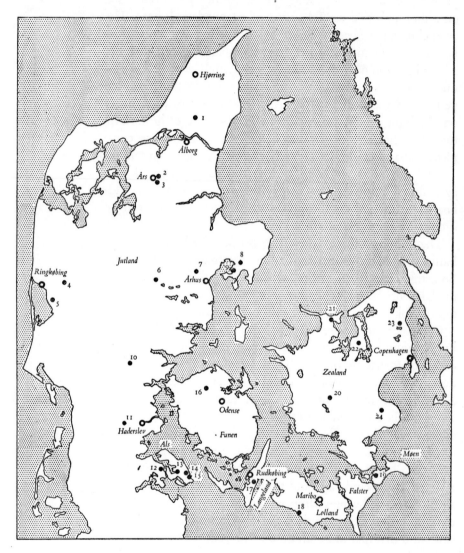

Fig. 16. Map of Denmark showing some important finding-places and museums.

ARCHAEOLOGICAL SITES

1. *Kraghede (cemetery, Pre-Roman Iron Age).*

2. *Gundestrup (silver cauldron, Pre-Roman Iron Age). (pl. 54, 55)*

3. *Borremose (fortification in a bog, Pre-Roman Iron Age).*

4. *Muldbjerg (Bronze Age tumulus, where male clothing was found). (pl. 33)*

5. *Dejbjerg (carts from Pre-Roman Iron Age).*

6. *Tollund (bog where Pre-Roman Iron Age man was found). (pl. 46)*

7 *Borum Eshøj (Bronze Age tumulus).*

8. *Barkær (Neolithic settlement).*

9. *Knebel (biggest dysse in Denmark).*

10. *Egtved (Bronze Age tumulus, where female clothing was found). (pl. 33)*

11. *Skrydstrup (Bronze Age tumulus). (pl. 31)*

12. *Nydam (bog where Late Roman Iron Age boat was found). (pl. 72)*

13. *Hjortspring (bog where Pre-Roman Iron Age boat was found). (pl. 49)*

14. *Oleskobbel (fine double long dysse).*

15. *Blommeskobbel (big long dysser).*

16. *Vimose (bog-find, Roman Iron Age).*

17. *Troldebjerg (Neolithic settlement).*

18. *Hoby (Early Roman Iron Age grave which yielded rich finds). (pl. 59)*

19. *Klekkendehøj (Giant's grave, double chamber)*

20. *Bromme (Palaeolithic settlement).*

21. *Trundholm (Sun-Chariot). (pl. 36)*

22. *Jægerspris (two fine giant's graves, Neolithic).*

23. *Kongedyssen (long dysse, Neolithic).*

24. *Himlingøje (cemetery, Late Roman Iron Age).*

25. *Madsebakke (rock-engravings, Bronze Age).*

26. *Gamleborg (hill-fort, Dark Age). (pl. 63)*

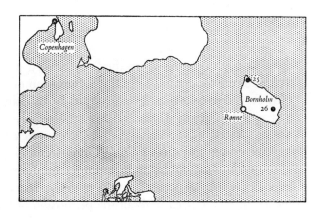

shelter and warmth at one end of the dwelling-house. The cold winds and snow of the winter must have been a considerable ordeal to these primitive peoples and we must presume that they welcomed the spring with rejoicing.

There were no drainage problems for the farms placed on sandy soil, but in the more clayey areas we notice that they are placed on gentle slopes which give a natural drainage to the fields and produce few water-logged patches.

The abandoned prehistoric fields are often difficult to find, being hidden in plantations or overgrown with heather and gorse. But once one has discovered them it is tempting to follow the system of banks and piles of stones that tell their own story of long-forgotten years of hard work.

Plates 10, 11, 19–21, 29–30

But it is the barrows, *dysser* and passage-graves that are most clearly visible in the countryside—over twenty-three thousand of them are protected by law. They are an integral part of the Danish landscape and have often formed the subject of paint-ings and engravings by Danish artists. Indeed, so great is their importance in the Danish landscape that they have appeared on bank-notes and on postage-stamps, while Hans Christian Andersen and Johannes V. Jensen have sung their praises. The barrows often serve as gazebos from which people may admire the sunset or view the surrounding countryside.

Some prehistoric monuments were saved at the beginning of the nineteenth century, when they were placed under the pro-tection of the Commission for the Preservation of Antiquities. However, destruction made more rapid strides than protection, and when at length it was realized how serious the situation was, a new law was introduced which protected all graves, settlement sites and earth-works. This law was introduced in 1937 and is administered through the National Museum. It pro-tects all ancient monuments in the countryside and no monu-ment can be removed without the permission of the National Museum. In this way graves and barrows, fields and settlement

sites are protected from the modern plough. While no compensation can be granted for a single protected monument, the
owner of a considerable protected area can be given a lump
sum in compensation. Decisions in these matters are reached
at the local County Committee. Every monument is inspected
at least once in every two or three years.

Protection on such a scale preserves prehistoric monuments
for the scholar and for the visitor, and there are few places in
Denmark which have no visible prehistoric remains. Some
parishes, indeed, have several hundred scheduled sites within
their boundaries. In north-western Zealand one is seldom far
from a *dysse* and even in the neighbourhood of Copenhagen
several good examples are to be found; at Tokkekøb hegn, one,
Kongedyssen (the king *dysse*), is beautifully preserved with
two chambers and tall kerb-stones. Rows of barrows can be
seen south of Tisvildeleje, and to the north-east of Århus lies
what is perhaps the largest *dysse* in Denmark, the impressive
Posekær Stenhus. The *dysser* on the island of Als are of
special interest, while those at Blommeskobbel and Oleskobbel
are probably the most imposing—several *dysser* can be found
in the island's forests. The woods of Bornholm conceal innumerable standing stones, two of the most impressive groups
being those at Louisenlund (Østermarie) and Gryet (Bodilsker). A ring of standing stones is to be seen in Skovgårds-
lunden (Bodilsker), while the outcrops of rock in northern
Bornholm bear rock-engravings. The largest collection of these
is to be found between Allinge and Sandvig on Madsebakke.
Passage-graves occur throughout the country and many are well
worth visiting. For instance, Jægerspris in north-western
Zealand can boast two passage-graves, one called Julianehøj, excavated in the late eighteenth century.

The National Museum and the Geodætisk Institut have published a series of archaeological maps (scale 1 : 100,000) which
are useful for a more detailed study of the visible monuments

Plate 29

137

of Danish prehistory. On these maps all the protected monuments are indicated together with the find-spots of the more important graves and objects. With the aid of these maps one can follow the coastline of the Ertebølle period, and see the oyster shells of the kitchen-middens shining white among the brown leaves that carpet the forest. One can pay a pilgrimage to the find-spot of the Gallehus horns, the Trundholm sun-chariot, the Dejbjerg carts, the Egtved woman or the Gundestrup cauldron. At each of the sites there is a stone to commemorate the discoveries of some of the greatest objects of Danish prehistory.

CHAPTER IX

Danefæ, Excavations and Collections

THE OLDEST LAW NOW VALID in Denmark concerns *Danefæ* (which means 'property of the dead'). It is based on the medieval law of the Danish provinces, on laws such as that described in Valdemar Sejr's Jutland Code of 1259: 'If any man find silver or gold in barrows or in the wake of his plough, it shall belong to the King.' Other laws from different parts of Denmark contain similar clauses, and the same regulation about *Danefæ* (property to which nobody has a legal claim) occurs in the laws of the first absolute King of Denmark. Royal decrees of 1737 and 1752 altered the simple wording of the original law and introduced an interpretation of *Danefæ* by which the objects were to be assessed not merely at their bullion value but at their antiquarian value. The decree of August 7, 1752 states:

> Although everything found buried in the earth, forests, fields, houses or any other place in the Land of Denmark, whether it be of gold, silver, metal or of any other treasure which no one claims, belongs as *Danefæ* to the King alone; an *ex gratia* award will be granted to any of those subjects who discover anything of this kind, so that he who finds coins or other objects, which on account of their antiquity or special nature can be considered a rarity, shall, if he despatch them to the Treasury, receive payment to their full value from the King's Purse.

This is an intriguing, if rambling, sentence but it clearly conveys its meaning despite the fact that it contrasts vividly with the sparing language of the older laws. Rarity and antiquity is of importance, apart from the metal value, and the King, through the Treasury, sees to it that the finder is adequately rewarded.

The wording of the 1752 decree is clearly influenced by other countries, and especially by Swedish laws, from which parts of the clause are directly taken. Objects claimed as *Danefæ* were brought together in the King's Art Collections and when these were dispersed in 1844–45 the National Museum received the *Danefæ*. Since that time the National Museum has administered the law and rewarded the finders with the full antiquarian value of the object according to the circumstances of the find.

It is not always easy to reconcile modern archaeological considerations with laws that are more than seven hundred years old. Flint, for instance, has never been listed as part of *Danefæ*, but this is due to the fact that there has never been a test case with regard to any particularly rare object in this material. On the whole, the National Museum tries to avoid drastic measures in the enforcement of this law, especially since the finders prove helpful and obliging. The Museum considers it to be of the greatest importance that the Danish people should view the archaeologist's work sympathetically and co-operate in the matter of reporting and recording finds, whether they be *Danefæ* or not. In the last hundred years *Danefæ* has seldom been wilfully concealed from the authorities, and when it has happened it has usually been done in ignorance. Such a case occurred recently, when a young farmer found a ring which he believed to be brass and used it to tie up cattle in the cow-shed! A visiting 'Vet.' recognized it as gold and submitted it, quite undamaged, to the National Museum, who dated it to the Bronze Age. The young finder, who had by then been called up for National Service, was agreeably surprised to receive a cheque for a considerable amount of money, completely tax-free as a result of the operation of the *Danefæ* law.

Many touching stories are told of the finders of *Danefæ*—how one was saved from bankruptcy and another enabled to buy a farm, and so on—for it is the finder and not the owner of the land who receives the compensation,

Valuable antiquities often come to light centuries later in strange circumstances: on one occasion a small boy tripped and fell, catching his foot in a heavy gold ring. This proved to be a unique piece worth a couple of hundred pounds in bullion value alone. A fisherman caught a rare neck-ring on his eel-spear, and another man, rowing off the coast of Jutland at Femø, saw the glitter of a gold ornament on the bed of the sea and managed to bring it to the surface. A large piece of gold was once rescued from a piece of peat burning in the fire, while recently, a heavy gold chain was revealed when a tree-root was cleared by blasting—unfortunately the object suffered severely in the process!

It is preferable that specialists should uncover and investigate archaeological finds, not only barrows, megalithic tombs and settlements, but also finds which may not seem very important at first sight. It is a popular misconception that excavation is an exciting and interesting form of amusement; whereas for the archaeologist it is much more a nerve-racking ordeal, since every new feature and find must be carefully studied, recorded and ultimately interpreted. A heavy responsibility rests on the leader of the excavation, and as the layers of earth are removed, so the evidence is destroyed and it is then impossible to correct any misinterpretations. An excavation may, on occasions, be exciting, but for the most part it is hard, painstaking and often uncomfortable—it is not every day that something interesting is revealed by the trowel or the brush.

The technique of excavation has, of course, progressed throughout the centuries, but excavation in the scientific spirit of enquiry started many years ago. We even have evidence that graves were disturbed in antiquity. In Denmark during the eighteenth and nineteenth centuries members of the Royal Family took an interest in excavation—Crown Prince Frederik investigated the barrow known as Julianehøj in 1776 and in

1824 Crown Prince Christian (later Christian VIII) excavated several sites including a hill-fort on Bornholm. Prince Frederik (later Frederik VII) was very much interested in archaeology and, often in collaboration with Worsaae, investigated a large number of barrows and even tried his hand on the large Jelling monument.

The first drawings of Danish excavations are those of Bishop Münter in the 1780's. During the nineteenth century the reports of excavations become more detailed and accurate; but it was not until the end of the nineteenth century that a fully satis-factory excavational technique was developed. The method of field work expounded in *Årbøger for nordisk Oldkyndighed og Historie* in 1897 was the result of consultation and team-work between the technicians and the archaeologists of the National Museum. Definite rules were laid down, and the importance of differentiating between the different layers or phases of a struc-ture was emphasized, for only in this manner can the relation-ship, say, of the different burials in a barrow be distinguished. According to these rules the excavation had to proceed with the greatest possible care so that every feature found could be recorded; all finds were to be photographed *in situ* and the plans were to be drawn to a fixed scale. In 1893 the National Museum received an annual grant of £500 for the furtherance of this work (a sum that would today be worth about £5,000). With this money many important excavations were carried out and the results published.

The Danish National Museum in Copenhagen, therefore, was mainly responsible for the development of archaeology in Denmark during the nineteenth and the early part of the twentieth century; it administered the law of *Danefæ*, protected ancient monuments and carried out the excavations. The result was a steady growth in its collections, so that it is now the most important museum for the study of Danish antiquities. All periods of prehistory are represented—here are to be seen the dagger from Hindgavl, the Trundholm sun-chariot, Bronze Age dress, the *lurer*, the Gundestrup cauldron, the Dejbjerg carts, the Hoby find and the weapons from Vimose, and a great deal besides. Apart from the many exhibits on view to the public, there are large reserve and study collections.

Plates 25, 36, 33, 44, 54, 55, and 59

But the National Museum is not the only one in Denmark. Even during the last century many of the provincial towns had their own small museums; today these museums have grown in size and many of them are run by staffs of specialists. There is the Forhistorisk Museum of the city and university of Århus, which contains the Grauballe man, the Brå cauldron and the great bog-find of Illerup. The Fyns Stiftsmuseum at Odense has an excellent collection of Iron Age finds, from the neigh-bourhood of Broholm, for instance; while the Vendsyssel Museum at Hjørring contains (among its other antiquities) bog-and grave-finds of the Early Iron Age. The museum at Hader-slev has a number of grave-finds from the Bronze and Iron Ages, as well as one of the Northern types of gold bowl. At Rønne, the capital of Bornholm, the museum houses a large collection of antiquities of all periods. Among the smaller museums one can instance Silkeborg, which contains the head of the Tollund man and Års, which houses a collection from the area of the Borremose fortification the same area that produced the Gundestrup cauldron. The Langeland Museum at Rudkøbing houses collections from the Stone Age settle-ments at Lindø and Troldebjerg. The museums at Ålborg, Thisted, Viborg, Randers, Sønderborg and Ringkøbing have collections which are well worth visiting, and even this does not exhaust them all. Furthermore, the policy of centralization built up during the last century is now being relaxed, so that people living in the provincial areas may develop a greater interest in their own antiquities.

Plate 48

Plate 46

Bibliography

J. Brøndsted, *Danmarks Oldtid*, vols. I–III, Copenhagen 1938–40, gives a thorough conspectus of the subject with a bibliography. Below is listed the more recent literature (to a large extent the papers quoted have English summaries).

Abbreviations: *Årb.: Årbøger for nordisk Oldkyndighed og Historie.*
                     Fra NM Arb.: Fra Nationalmuseets Arbejdsmark.
                     Acta Arch.: Acta Archaeologica.

GENERAL

S. Müller, *Nationalmuseet*, Copenhagen 1907. Glyn E. Daniel, *A Hundred Years of Archaeology*, London 1950.

THE PALAEOLITHIC

Hollerup: U. Møhl, *Årb.* 1954. Th. Mathiassen, *Årb.* 1946. J. Troels-Smith, *Fra NM Arb.* 1955.

THE MESOLITHIC

Artifacts: Th. Mathiassen, *Danish Antiquities*, vol. I, Copenhagen 1948. Star Carr: J. G. D. Clark, *Excavations at Star Carr*, Cambridge 1954. Houses: K. Andersen, *Fra NM Arb.* 1951. Settlement sites at Kloster-lund and Gudenå: Th. Mathiassen, *Årb.* 1937. General literature: Th. Mathiassen, *Stenaldersbopladser i Åmosen*, 1943, and *Dyrholmen*, 1942. E. Westerby, *Stenaldersbopladser ved Klampenborg*, 1927. Hafted microlith: M. Petersson, *Meddelanden från Lunds universitets historiska museum*, 1951. Fish-trap: M. Petersson, *ibid.*, 1952.

THE NEOLITHIC

Artifacts: P. V. Glob, *Danish Antiquities*, vol. II, Copenhagen 1952. The beginning of the Neolithic: C. J. Becker, *Årb.* 1947 and 1954. J. Troels-Smith, *Årb.* 1953. Finds from *dysser*: K. Thorvildsen, *Årb.* 1941.

Grønhøj: K. Thorvildsen, *Årb.* 1946. Tustrup: P. Kjærum, *Kuml*, 1955. The Single-Grave culture: P. V. Glob, *Studier i den jyske Enkeltgravkultur*, 1944. Bundsø: Th. Mathiassen, *Årb.* 1939.

THE BRONZE AGE

Artifacts: H. C. Broholm, *Danish Antiquities*, vols. III–IV, Copenhagen 1952–53. The finds are published in H. C. Broholm, *Danmarks Bronze-alder*, vols. I–IV, Copenhagen 1943–49. General literature: H. C. Broholm, W. P. Larsen and G. Skjerne, *The Lures of the Bronze Age*, Copenhagen 1949. H. C. Broholm and Margrethe Hald, *Costumes of the Bronze Age of Denmark*, Copenhagen 1940. Bird's wings in urn burial: H. Winge, *Vidensk. Medd. fra den naturhist. Forening i København*, 1904. The Vixø helmets: H. Norling-Christensen, *Acta Arch.* XVII, 1946. The Næstved find: H. C. Broholm, *Årb.* 1954.

THE PRE-ROMAN IRON AGE

O. Klindt-Jensen, *Bronzekedelen fra Brå*, Århus 1953, and Foreign influences in Denmark's Early Iron Age, *Acta Arch.* XX, 1949. C. J. Becker, *Acta Arch.* XIX, 1948. G. Rosenberg, *Hjortspringfundet*, 1937. House at Gørding: H. Andersen, *Kuml*, 1951. E. Albrectsen, *Fynske jernaldergrave* I, 1954. Iron Age textiles: M. Hald, *Olddanske Textiler*, 1950. Ploughs: P. V. Glob, *Ard og Plov*, Århus 1951. Two British coins: R. Thomsen, *Fra NM Arb.* 1953.

THE ROMAN IRON AGE

O. Klindt-Jensen, Foreign Influences (see above). H. Norling-Christensen, *Katalog over Ældre Romersk Jærnalders Grave i Århus Amt*, Copenhagen 1954, and *Acta Arch.* XIX, 1948. J. Werner, *Die beiden Zierscheiben des Thorsberger Moorfundes*, 1941. J. Brøndsted, *Guldhornene*, 1954. O. Voss and M. Ørsnes-Christensen, *Acta Arch.* XIX, 1948. Illerup: H. Andersen, *Kuml*, 1951. E. Albrectsen, *Fynske Jernaldergrave* II, 1956, and *Årb*, 1946. General literature about Roman imports: H. J. Eggers, *Der römische Import im freien Germanien*, 1951.

THE DARK AGE

M. Mackeprang, *De nordiske Guldbrakteater*, Århus 1952. O. Klindt⁄
Jensen, *Bornholm i folkevandringstiden*, Copenhagen 1957. Recent hoards:
O. Voss, *Acta Arch.* xxv, 1954. E. Munksgård, *Acta Arch.* xxvi, 1955.
H. Norling⁄Christensen, *Viking* xiii, 1949. The Kyndby cemetery:
M. Ørsnes⁄Christensen, *Acta Arch.* xxvi, 1955.

THE PREHISTORIC LANDSCAPE

Th. Mathiassen, *Studier over Vestjyllands Oldtidsbebyggelse*, 1948. P. V.
Glob, *Danske Oldtidsminder*, 1948.

DANEFÆ

S. Müller, *Nationalmuseet*, 1907, V. Nielsen, *Juristen*, 1950.

SOURCES OF ILLUSTRATIONS

With the exception of four, kindly supplied by Dr Iversen (8),
Mr Kjaerum (14, 17) and Mr Harald Andersen (61), the original
photographs came either from the archives of the National Museum,
Copenhagen, or were specially taken for this book by Mr L. Larsen,
photographer at the National Museum.

The figures derive in part from material at the National Museum. The
flint implements are based on Th. Mathiassen, *Danish Antiquities* vol. i,
Copenhagen 1948. Figures 7, 8 are from C. J. Becker, *Årb.* 1947;
figure 11 from O. Klindt⁄Jensen, *Bornholm i folkevandringstiden*, 1957;
figures 12, 13 from P. V. Glob, *Fra NM Årb.* 1946; figure 14 from
O. Klindt⁄Jensen, *Årb.* 1952, and B. Salin, *Die altgermanische Thierorna⁄
mentik*, 1904; figure 15 from B. Salin, *ibid.*

THE PLATES

2

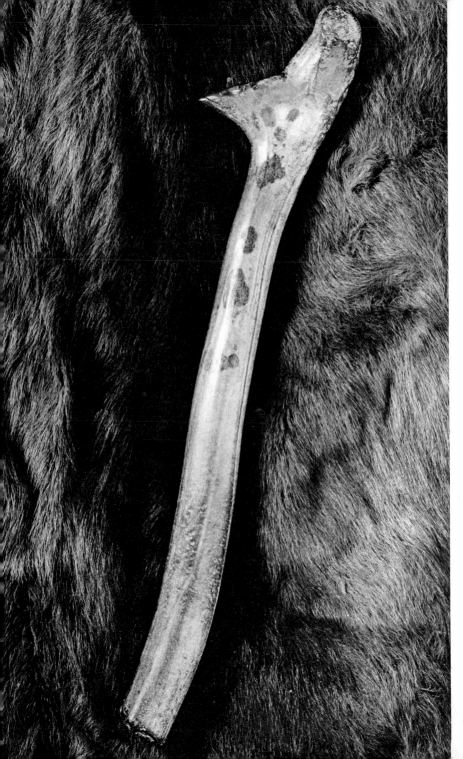

4

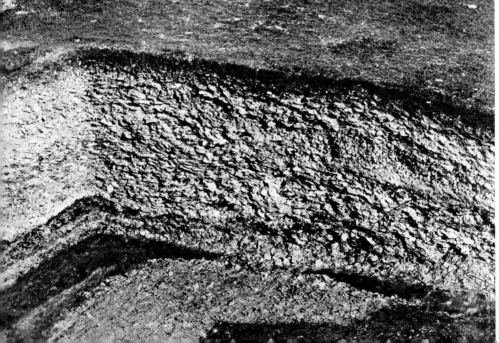

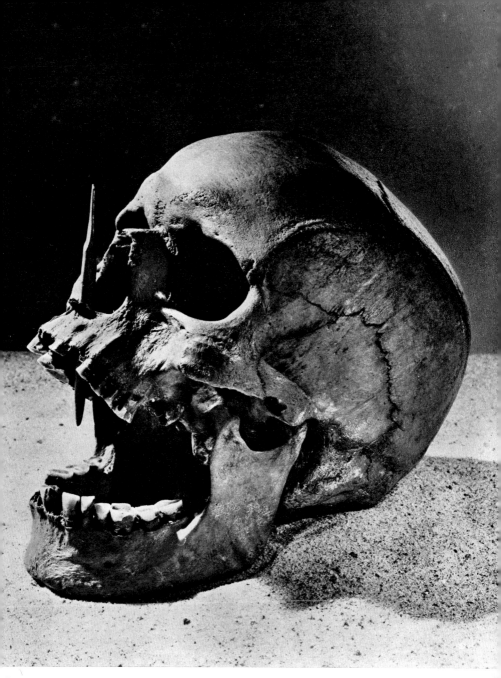

8

24

31

32

33

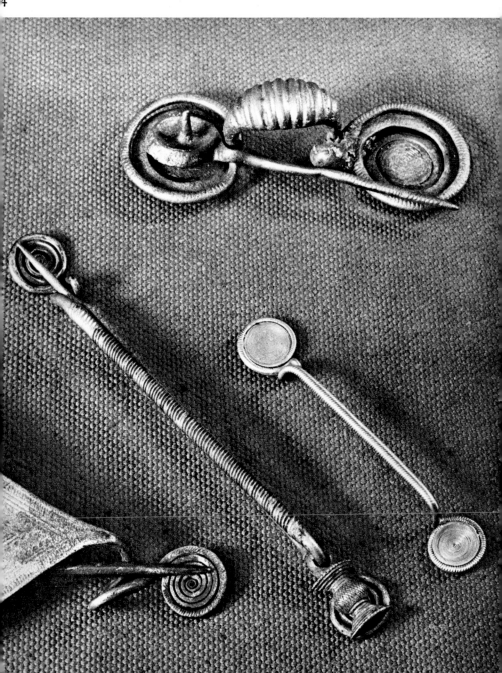

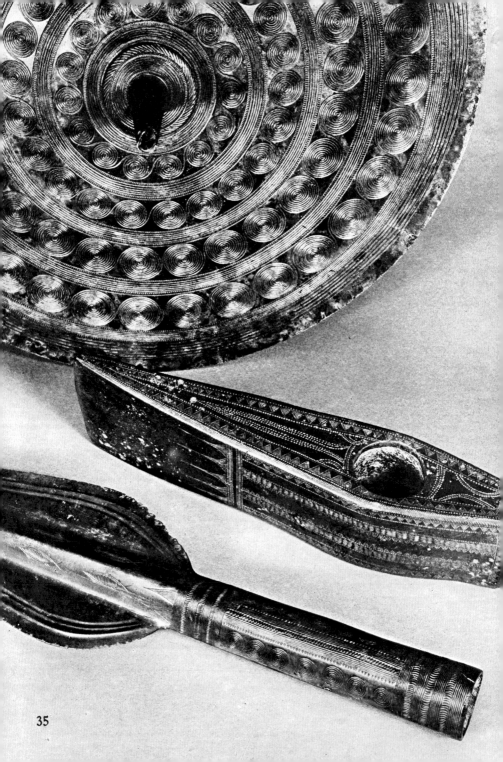

38

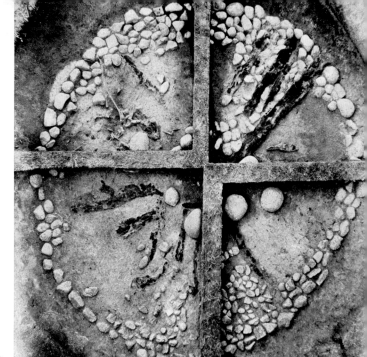

42

43

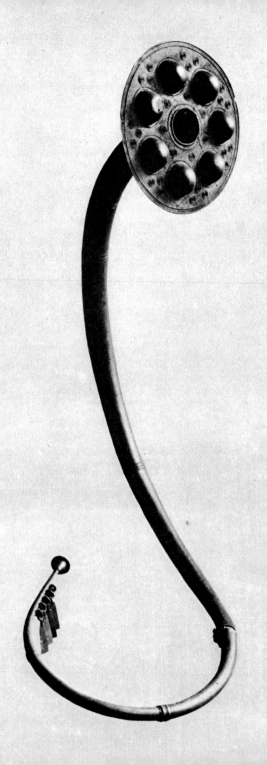

44

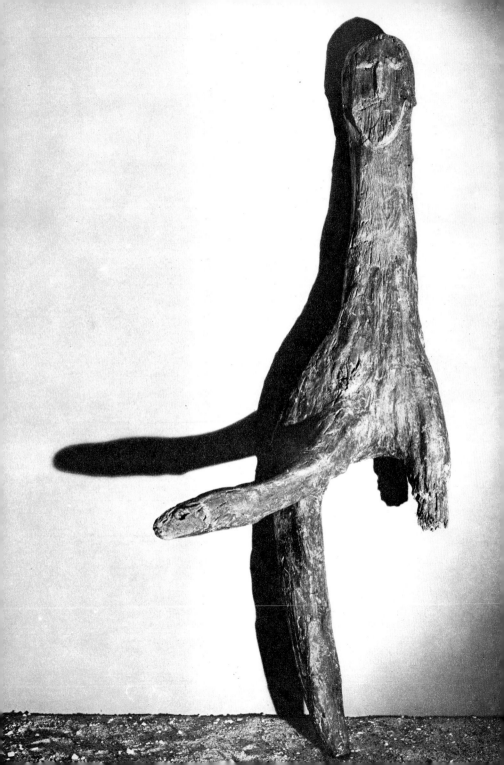

48

49

50

51

54

55

56

60

63

64

66

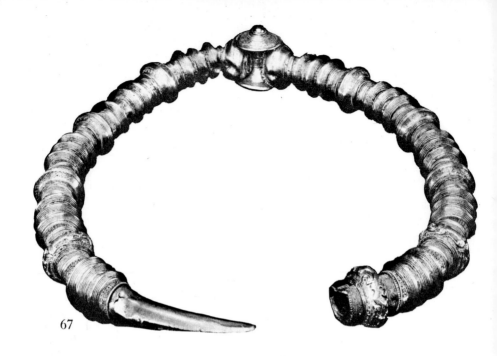

67

68

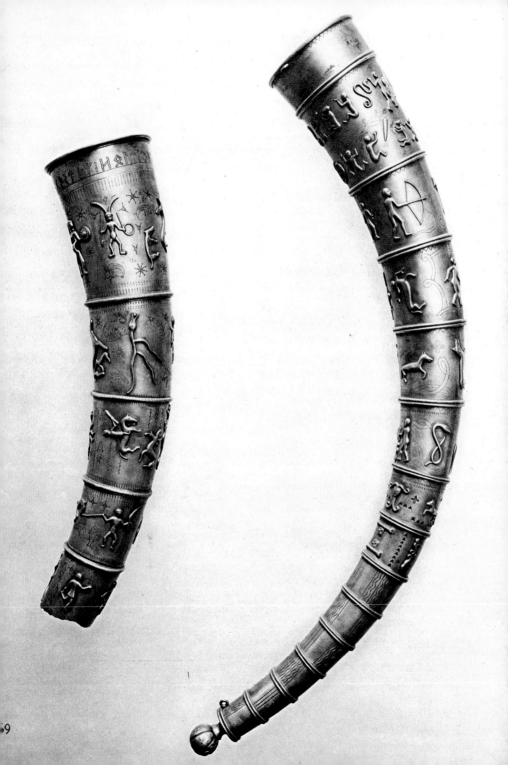

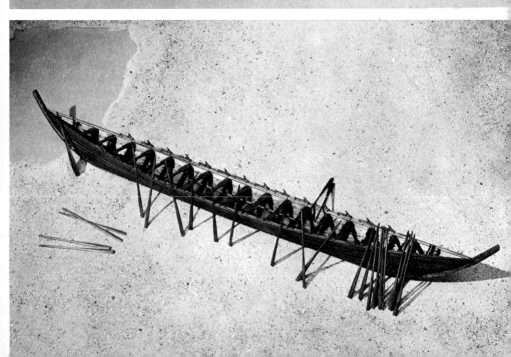

NOTES ON THE PLATES

Notes on the Plates

1   J. J. A. Worsaae. (Drawing by A. Jerndorf.)

2   Sophus Müller. (Sketch by P. C. Krøyer.)

3   C. J. Thomsen showing the Old Nordic Museum to the public. In his hands he has one of the big golden rings from Broholm, South Funen. (Drawing by Magnus Petersen 1846.)

4   Reindeer-antler axe from the vicinity of Odense (on a reindeer hide). 2:5.

5   Top left: amber bear from Resen, Central Jutland. Centre: two bone points from Trørød and Slangerup, north of Copenhagen, and amber elk head from Egemarke, West Zealand. Bottom: ornamented bones from Ryemarkgård, Zealand. Right: harpoon-head from Løjesmølle bog, Zealand. 3:4.

6   View from the mesolithic settlement of Hestekleven near Årsdale, Bornholm. Pines may have grown there since the Stone Age.

7   Section through the kitchen-midden of Ertebølle, North Jutland; photo of the excavation about 1900.

8   Modern clearing-fire in a wood of foliiferous trees near Draved, South Jutland.

9   Thin-butted flint axe in the stem of an oak tree, which was felled with this stone implement (it took about an hour). The shaft is a modern copy.

10, 11   *Dysser*, at Vilsted, Zealand.

12 Grave at Forum, West Jutland. The skeleton has disappeared.

13 Find consisting of vessels and a mace head from a grave under a barrow in Tovstrup near Ringkøbing, West Jutland. 1:3.

14 Pottery from the sacrificial building at Tustrup, East Jutland. (see 17)

15 Pottery from the middle of the Neolithic period: a hanging-pot, a big biconical and a cylindrical vessel and ladle. They are from the Megalithic culture; except the cylindrical pot, which was found in a passage-grave near Hagebrogård, Jutland, 1:3.

16 Two trepanned skulls from megalithic graves. The nearer one, from Næs, Falster, shows a healed wound.

17 View of the sacrificial building at Tustrup, East Jutland. The big stones have been set up.

18 Skull of a man who has been killed by arrows. A bone point has pierced the nose. From Porsmose near Næstved, South Zealand.

19 Passage-grave (*jættestue*) in Frejlev wood, Lolland.

20 Interior of a typical Danish passage-grave. Left, the entrance.

21 View of single-grave barrows at Almind, Central Jutland.

22 Single-grave (under-grave) of a woman, whose amber beads can be seen in front of her head. Near Torupgårde, Alslev, West Jutland.

23 Single-Grave culture types. Beaker and battle-axe from (left) Møbjerggård, East Jutland (under-grave); (centre) Slauggård near Vorbasse, East Jutland (bottom-grave); (right) Østbirk near Horsens, East Jutland (over-grave). App. 1:4.

24   Vessel with eyes, nose and brows from Svinø (Køng parish). Megalithic culture. 2:3.

25   Flint dagger from Hindsgavl. Late Neolithic. 2:3.

26   Left: imported bronze dagger from Jutland together with a Danish copy in flint. Right: a bronze slashing sword from West Zealand and its Danish counterpart in flint from Faurskov, Funen. 2:5.

27   Bronze swords and daggers. From left to right: Hungarian sword (from Torupgard, Lolland) and Danish sword (from Valsømagle, Zealand), both Earliest Bronze Age. Danish dagger from Gjedsted, Central Jutland (period II); sword from Ejsing, West Jutland, and dagger from Breum, Central Jutland (period III). 1:5.

28   Cast finds. Implements for casting and remains of a bronze moulding (top left) and a crucible (top right).

29   A row of Bronze Age barrows, North Zealand.

30   A barrow, presumably Bronze Age. Højby, North-west Zealand.

31   The Skrydstrup coffin in its barrow under excavation.

32   The Egtved coffin opened in the laboratory.

33   Left: male clothing from Borum Eshøj, East Jutland. Right: female clothing from Egtved, East Jutland.

34   Brooches of bronze and gold. From left to right: part of a Bornholm brooch (period III); a period II and a period III bronze brooch. Top: a period IV bronze brooch. 5:4.

35   Ornamentation. Top: part of the Langstrup belt ornament (period II);

centre: a richly decorated bronze axe (period I). Bottom: part of the Valsømagle spear-head (period I). 2:3.

36 The Trundholm sun-chariot, North-west Zealand.

37 From the big hoard of Røgerup, North Zealand (period IV). Two neck-rings, three pins and a curled ornament. 2:5.

38 Bronze belt-boxes. Right: from period IV. Middle and left: from period V.

39 Imports in the Late Bronze Age. Centre: one of the two helmets from Vixø, Zealand. Bottom left: an 'antenne' sword. Behind: a bronze shield. 2:5.

40 Part of the excavation of Mandhøj, Bornholm. A section through the barrow with the remains of the mortuary house (cf. plate 42 and fig. 11).

41 Cist in the middle of a barrow, with cremated bones and a sword. Middle Bronze Age.

42 The remains of a mortuary house at Mandhøj (cf. plate 40 and fig. 11).

43 Late Bronze Age urn in a section through one of the barrows at Mandhøj.

44 *Lur* from Brudevælte, North Zealand, period V. 1:6.

45 Razor with a ship design and small ornamentations. 1:1.

46 The head of the Tollund man.

47 Wooden male sculpture from Broddenbjerg, North Jutland. App. 1:3.

48 Owl's head on a fitment of the Brå cauldron, East Jutland. 1:1.

49 Model of the Hjortspring boat.

50 Pottery from a skeleton grave at Enekrogen, Bornholm. Early Roman Iron Age. 1:5.

51 Danish neck⁻ring with Celtic *triskele* design from Gammelborg, Møen. Pre⁻Roman Iron Age. 5:6.

52 View of road at Tibirke, North Zealand. Pre⁻Roman Iron Age.

53 The excavation of the road at Broskov, South Zealand. Roman Iron Age.

54 Inner plate of the Gundestrup cauldron. Pre⁻Roman Iron Age. App. 2:5.

55 The Gundestrup cauldron. App. 1:5.

56 Skeleton grave from Bulbjerg cemetery, East Jutland. Roman Iron Age.

57 Detail of the female skeleton in one of the rich Juellinge graves, Lolland. Silver pins with gold granulation can be seen. In her hand (wearing a gold finger⁻ring) she holds a Roman sieve. Three brooches are lying on the shoulders and on the breast.

58 From the Dollerup double⁻grave: two silver goblets and two drinking⁻ horns with bronze mountings (the horns themselves are imitations). 1:3.

59 From the Hoby grave. Two silver goblets, a bronze vase and a big bronze disc. 1:3.

60 Imports. Late Roman glassware from Himlingøje, Zealand (centre and right) and a glass vase from the Dark Age (left).

61 From the bog⁻find at Illerup, East Jutland. Spear⁻heads, a comb, etc.

62 The loom-weights in House II, Sorte Muld, Bornholm, lying in a row just as they were hanging. App. 1:5.

63 Hill-fort at Gamleborg, Bornholm.

64 Grave at Donbæk, North Jutland. Dark Age.

65 Two gold neck-rings with punched ornamentation, and a gold bracteate (C-type). App. 3:4.

66 Wooden sculpture from Rude Eskildstrup, Zealand. The figure has a triple gold neck-ring, one of which is like the one in plate 67. 1:3.

67 Gold neck-ring from Falster. 1:2.

68 Gold *gubber* ('gaffers') from Bornholm. 2:1.

69 The two golden horns from Gallehus, South Jutland. App. 1:3.

70 The Dalshøj hoards: seventeen gold coins from the late Roman Empire, a silver-gilt brooch and four gold pieces. 5:6.

71 Bronze ornament in the shape of a horse. A little more than 1:1.

72 A model of the Nydam boat.

73 Dark Age ornamentation: two birds with snakes. Garnets in gilt bronze. 3:2.

Index

Core-axe, Early Neolithic, 44
Cornwall, tin from, 58
Cortaillod culture of Switzerland, 35
Cremation: Bronze Age, 71, 72, 76; Pre-
Roman Iron Age, 82–6, 98
Crested pelican, 37
Crevens Vaenge, South Zealand, Bronze
Age figures from, 78–9

Daggers: Mesolithic, 29; Middle Neo-
lithic, 56; Late Neolithic, 56; Bronze
Age, 60
Dalshøj, Roman Iron Age houses at, 114,
115
Danefae, 139–40
Danes, raid the West, 120–1
Dead, cult of the: Middle Neolithic, 49–50;
Bronze Age, 63
See also Soul
Dejbjerg, West Jutland, Pre-Roman Iron
Age vehicles from, 88–9
Dogs, in the Dark Age, 127
Domestic ware, Roman Iron Age, 103–6,
110–11
Domesticated animals: Middle Neolithic,
47; Roman Iron Age, 116; Dark Age,
127
Dollerup, East Jutland, Roman Iron Age
objects from, 105
Donnerplund, Jutland, Pre-Roman Iron
Age *ard* from, 94, 97
Døstrup, Jutland, Pre-Roman Iron Age
ard from, 94
Drinking-horns, Roman Iron Age, 105
Drinking sets, Roman Iron Age, 103–6
Ducks, 37

Dyrholmen, East Jutland, Mesolithic
settlement at, 32; evidence of Neolithic
cannibalism at, 36
Dysser. See Graves
Early Coast culture. *See* Ertebølle culture
Eastern Roman Empire, 119
Egtved, East Jutland, Bronze Age grave
at, 64
Elburz Mountains, earliest agricultural
settlement in, 34
Elk, 36, 37
settlement in, 34
Ertebølle culture, 30–3, 36, 39, 43–5
Eskimos, 43
Etruscan bronze vessel, 99

Fallow-deer, 14
Fårdal, North Jutland, Bronze Age
animal heads from, 78
Farm-sites, Dark Age, 126–9
Fauna: Late Glacial period, 16, 18; Meso-
lithic, 22; eradication of elks and
aurochs during Early Neolithic period,
36; Neolithic, 37
Fertility cults: Bronze Age, 79–80; Pre-
Roman Iron Age, 94
Fields, Pre-Roman Iron Age, 95–6
Fish-hooks: Early Neolithic, 43; Middle
Neolithic, 54; Bronze Age, 60
Fish-spear, Early Neolithic, 43
Fishing-nets, Early Neolithic, 43
Fjand, West Jutland, Roman Iron Age
houses at, 114, 115, 117
Flake-axe, Early Neolithic, 44
Flakes, flaking: Late Glacial period, 17;
Early Neolithic, 39; Middle Neolithic, 46

207